16-99

■ *Virginia Lynn Fry* ■

Part of Me Died, Too

STORIES OF CREATIVE SURVIVAL AMONG BEREAVED CHILDREN AND TEENAGERS

With a Foreword by Katherine Paterson

DUTTON CHILDREN'S BOOKS
■ NEW YORK ■

Library of Congress Cataloging-in-Publication Data
Fry, Virginia. Part of me died, too: stories of creative survival
among bereaved children and teenagers / Virginia Lynn Fry;
illustrated with the children's own artwork, with a foreword by
Katherine Paterson.—1st ed.   p.   cm.   ISBN 0-525-45068-8
1. Bereavement in children—Juvenile literature.   2. Bereavement
in youth—Juvenile literature.   I. Paterson, Katherine.   II. Title.
BF723.G75F79   1995   155.9'37'083—dc20
94-36536   CIP   AC

Published in the United States 1995
by Dutton Children's Books,
a division of Penguin Books USA Inc.
375 Hudson Street, New York, New York 10014
Designed by Adrian Leichter
Printed in Hong Kong
First Edition
10   9   8   7   6   5   4   3   2   1

FOR ALL CHILDREN WHO SEARCH FOR THOSE
WHO ARE MISSING—MAY THE GRIEF PASS ON THROUGH
AND EMERGE INTO HEALING.

You can't prevent the birds of sorrow from flying overhead,
but you can keep them from building nests in your hair.

CHINESE PROVERB

CONTENTS

In 1974, when our son David was eight years old, his best friend, Lisa, was struck and killed by lightning. It was not the first time our children had come face-to-face with death—a child in Mary's nursery school had died suddenly three years before—but it was the first death of someone they had felt really close to. David was totally devastated. He reasoned that somehow Lisa's death must have been his fault. His father and I tried to comfort him, but we seemed unable to.

Lisa's grandmother, even in the midst of her own sorrow, realized the extent of David's grief. She asked us to find something that might help David that could be her gift to him.

My husband, John, suggested that we use Mrs. Hill's gift to get clay lessons for David. He knew a potter nearby who was a gentle and wise person and asked her if she would be willing to give David private sessions. Those lessons proved to be the most comforting thing that happened to David during that terrible period of his life.

The first time I met Virginia Fry, I thought immediately of the potter who had meant so much to David. As I listened to her speak about the grieving children with whom she was working, I was thrilled. Here in our own community was a wise and gentle young woman who had chosen to use her artistic gift to help children survive devastating experiences. She was doing intentionally the kind of therapy we had sensed a need for back in 1974.

We Americans on the whole aren't very good with death. We are all going to die, but we do everything we can to deny the fact. We parents try our best to protect our children from sorrow, and when we can't, we tell ourselves that they aren't old enough to understand death or able to feel intense loss. So we leave our children alone with their questions unanswered, their grief raw and unassuaged.

As you will see when you read this book, Virginia Fry takes the grief of children seriously and spends her life and her considerable talent helping them express that grief in ways that heal rather than destroy.

These are not easy stories to read. They are sad, even tragic, stories, but they are true. They have happened to real children, and, though we would never choose for the young to suffer, similar events have happened and will happen to many other children. For them and for those who care for them, this book can be a light in a very dark place, an instrument for creative survival, just as Virginia herself has been and continues to be for the children she works with in central Vermont. I wish we had known her in Maryland in 1974. I am grateful that we know her now.

KATHERINE PATERSON
Barre, Vermont

The struggle to understand loss and death in a healthy manner began for me when I was twenty-seven and my younger brother David died suddenly in a truck accident. He was twenty-one. The phone call from my father at five o'clock in the morning changed my life forever. There would be no opportunity for good-byes, no further chances to listen more carefully, to laugh more fully, to enjoy David's incredible spirit and daredevil nerve one last time. The bottom dropped out from under me. As I flew to his funeral in the Arizona mountains, I felt adrift in deep, black space.

My family groped for something to do when nothing could be done. We were artists, so we turned to what was familiar: We expressed our horror at losing David and the stabbing pain of missing him through our various creative outlets.

My oldest brother made a collage of David's life for the funeral service, so we all could focus on who he was. My youngest brother turned his nightmares into drawings and etchings, which defused his fears and anger, and helped him accept the good and bad of

David's lost life. My mother, looking for clues, for pieces of David's soul in what he loved, listened to every record she could find amid the jumble of his possessions. The tapes she made of special songs became the "David Tapes," a comfort in her saddest moments. My unathletic father honored David's energetic spirit by taking up jogging with my mother. In the pain of working with their own bodies, their pain at losing a child seemed to subside, if only momentarily.

And me? I wrote everything I could remember about David in my journal—our last conversations, his fears about the future, my distress over his death, and the sudden togetherness of my family. I painted "A Caged Bird," a work David had always urged me toward but which I had never attempted. Then I painted the bird again, but this time escaping its cage, as I felt David's troubled spirit had escaped our world for the next. All of these things brought me comfort. They transferred the grief from my body onto paper or canvas.

But it took nearly three years for me to realize that my grieving was unfinished. A doctor who was helping me figure out why I got sick so often asked me, "What is undone about your brother's death?" I had already gone back to Arizona and climbed David's favorite mountain, where we scattered his ashes. And I had cried more than I ever thought I could. So what *was* left?

Then I knew—David's portrait! To draw that beautiful, joking, devil-may-care face one more time. But could I do it from memory? I had never drawn that way before. I set about gathering photos and stories from my family and his friends until his presence was clear inside me. Then I drew in charcoal. First the eyes came. But an artist never begins with the eyes, and it seemed scary to have him watch me draw. I cried as I drew—but I got the drawing out, and it was David. His college friends were moved to tears and laughter by my drawing. And I was relieved to be free from the sadness that had gripped me inside and made me sick.

The impact of David's death and my process of healing left me restless. I was anxious to do more with my art than paint. In my search for a way to bring medicine and art together, I discovered the groundbreaking work that hospices were doing in caring for the terminally ill and their families.

At the outset, my role as a hospice artist was to help people be creative in the last days and months of their lives, to help them leave behind their gifts of love and find peace and comfort in the process. While doing this, I met children watching family members die. As a distraction from the tension and sadness, we began doing drawings together. Our busy hands made it easy to talk about what was happening to their families. Their art gave voice and clarity to their feelings. The opportunity for creative expression allowed the wise understanding inside these beautiful children to emerge and carry them through the crisis of death.

The stories in this book are true stories of children I have worked with. They are stories of the deaths and losses they experienced and the creative strategies they used to survive and heal their grief. Nearly all of the chapters have been reviewed by the children involved—now three to twelve years older. They are proud of their willingness to struggle, of their efforts to understand, of their desire to lead happy lives. As they move into adult life—graduating from school, starting to work, or getting married —without their deceased family members to witness these transitions, they experience the losses they endured as children yet again, in new ways.

I will always miss my brother David, but now I know his death will not keep me from living a happy life. He would not have wanted that. Each person in my family, and in any family that loses a loved one, has to make a decision to go on and truly live well. That decision is not possible without facing what has been lost, without observing how the meaning of a death changes as we grow. The children in these chapters tried, and are still trying, to do that. They, and I, hope that their explorations will help others.

ACKNOWLEDGMENTS

I am very grateful to the wonderful, amazing young people and their courageous families with whom I witnessed these intimate experiences of dying and living. And I thank them for allowing me to share their lessons in creative survival with other children, teenagers, and their families.

I could not have done this work without the support, insight, and excellent care of my first hospice-team members: Linda Kilburn, Elinor Robinson, Sheila Flynn Scott, Sandy Skelly Skinner, Pat Booth, Bernice Grodman, and Pat Daoust. I offer my thanks and greatest respect to hospice leader Diana Peirce, who enables me to continue this work with children in Vermont, and to all the other fantastic people who care for the dying through hospice work.

The kids' grief support groups could not have become the safe and loving explorations that they were without co-leaders Laine Gifford and my friend, colleague, and confidant, Kate Leonard.

This book owes much to the sensitive wisdom and persistent

dedication of my editor, Donna Brooks. Her determination that children need not grow up forced into terrifying silence and darkness, where death is concerned, brought this book to light. And I thank Katherine Paterson for her beam of hope and encouragement throughout the writing process.

Finally, and from the beginning, I am eternally grateful for the creative and loving family I was born into, and for the buoyant one I am raising now with my wise and patient husband, Mark Fitzsimmons.

Part of Me Died, Too

Has there been a death in your family? This book is about how children of different ages have dealt with the death of a parent, sister, brother, or other relative or friend. The youngest child in the book is a year and a half old; the oldest adolescent is eighteen. You can read the chapters alone or with a parent, teacher, or with other kids who know what it is like to feel lost inside because someone you love has died. Or you can read this book even if you have never experienced the death of someone close to you, but want to learn more about the feelings of loss and grief.

The chapters progress from the earliest losses most of us experience to losses of a more complex and difficult nature—deaths from AIDS, suicide, and murder. You can read the chapters in any order that appeals to you. Each one emphasizes different aspects of loss and survival. You needn't have experienced each loss to find the stories helpful to yourself or to someone you may know.

You may want to keep a pencil and paper nearby so that as you read, you can try out some of the activities suggested in each chapter. The creative survival strategies are meant to help us grieve, but they are also useful ways to help us enjoy life. You may get ideas for your own creative strategies—working with paper, markers, or clay can be fun. And the strategies can help you with other kinds of losses, too—divorce, accidents, or changes in friendships, schools, or finances.

What this book will *not* do is take away all the pain from your loss. The goal of grieving, and of this book, is not to make the loss go away. It is to make us aware of the feelings that the loss brings up in us, to help keep those feelings moving through us. Grief that is stuck makes us feel that we are only existing—not really alive, not free to enjoy life.

This is also a book for adults, because when it comes to death, most of us are still kids. Our first reaction to loss is: What's going to happen to me? Truly grieving over our losses takes everything we've got, including a sense of humor. As a hospice graffiti board reads, "Death sucks. Sorrow floats. And stomachs rule. When do we eat?"

Liam & Mac

Death of a Pet

Liam wrapped his little arms tightly around his mother's neck as they looked into the back of the pickup truck. His beloved dog, Mac, was lying there, but Mac's big black body was still. Liam's father touched Mac and called his name, but Mac didn't respond. The gentle, bounding spirit that had animated this great dog was gone.

Liam, too, reached out to touch the dog. Mac's fur was soft, but the body underneath felt stiff and lifeless. Liam drew back his hand and wound it into his mother's hair. The three of them stood there looking at the dog that had been their good friend and family member. It was hard to believe Mac was dead.

In his prime, Mac had been a ninety-pound Doberman with floppy ears and a gentle disposition. He loved everyone. He never barked or nipped, even when someone played roughly with him. He just allowed himself to be tossed and tumbled about, licking a face in the midst of the roughhousing whenever he got a chance. Mac ran like the wind and could make beautiful twisting leaps six feet into the air to catch a Frisbee between his teeth.

Mac had been the pet of Liam's dad, Mark, for five years. When Mark married Ginny, Mac became their dog. Mac wore a crown of flowers at their wedding and sniffed all the presents with good-humored curiosity.

After Liam was born and Mark and Ginny brought him home from the hospital, Mac licked the baby from head to toe. He became Liam's foremost protector. Whenever Mac walked by, he would give Liam a quick lick, as though to reassure the baby that all was well. Liam grew as familiar with the feel of Mac's tongue as he was with his mama's kisses and his daddy's hugs.

When Liam was learning to walk, Mac would lie down next to him so the baby could pull himself up on Mac's fur. Liam would cruise around Mac, grabbing little fistfuls of fur for balance. Mac didn't seem to mind. Interested and unflinching, he would follow Liam with his eyes. If he occasionally decided he had had enough, he would stand up slowly, slide Liam to the floor, and walk away.

When Liam was one and a half years old, Mac started to cough. It was a dry sound, deep and loud. The cough didn't go away, so the veterinarian came to the house to see what was wrong. After listening to Mac and examining him, she told Mark and Ginny that Mac had "kennel cough." She explained that large dogs sometimes developed trouble with their lungs as they got older. Their hearts could not pump enough blood to the lungs to oxygenate their big bodies for more than seven or eight years. The vet gave Mac some medicine, and for a few days he sounded better.

But after a week, Mac began to cough again. He lay on his side and breathed rapidly, seemingly unable to stand. Mark knew he had to take Mac to the vet right away. He carried the huge dog out to the truck and put him down on a blanket in the back. From his mother's arms, Liam gave Mac a pat. Then the whole family got into the truck and drove off. The animal hospital was only ten minutes away, but when Mark opened the back of the pickup, Mac didn't move. He didn't lift his head or flutter an eyelid. There was no sign of breath in his chest.

Liam reached out to Mac again, patting his dog with a puzzled look. The vet came out of the hospital and examined Mac, as Liam's parents watched sadly. She shook her head and explained that Mac had died of congestive heart failure. His heart had become too weak to pump blood to his lungs, so both organs had filled up with fluid and stopped working. They talked about what to do with Mac's large body. The soil in Mark and Ginny's backyard covered a rocky ledge. It was too shallow to permit them to bury Mac there.

The vet offered to have Mac's body cremated, and the cremains, or "ashes," placed in a special part of her field. Mark and Ginny knew that all bodies—animals' and people's—go back to being part of the earth eventually. But not all bodies are buried. Some people choose to have the bodies of their dead loved ones cremated, or decomposed by very intense heat. The bodies, sometimes enclosed in a casket and sometimes not, are put in a small space that can be made very hot. There is no actual flame or burning. The heat is so high that the body essentially vaporizes, until only bones are left. These are ground down into small bits that can be buried in the earth or scattered in an ocean or a garden, or whatever a family chooses to do with them. Ginny and Mark would bury Mac's cremains, and they would become part of the earth on which he had loved to run.

Mark and Ginny were shocked and upset about Mac's sudden death. They forgot that Liam was also observing Mac's dead body and the discussion about cremation. Not yet two, he wasn't talking yet, and at the vet's he was quiet and well behaved. It was easy to assume he didn't understand what was happening.

Later that afternoon Ginny was washing out Mac's bowls for the last time and packing them away in a cardboard box. Liam began tugging at her legs, pointing to the box. He chattered insistently, gesturing from the box to the place by the refrigerator where Mac's bowls usually belonged. Liam looked scared and angry. He knew something was not right. His gestures seemed to say the bowls should go back where they had always been—in the corner, not in the box. Suddenly his mother understood. Liam realized that a change was taking place, a change that involved the loss of a loved one. He needed an explanation. Ginny wiped her tears, got down on her knees, and put an arm around him.

"Liam, Mac died. Mac is dead. When animals die they don't eat anymore, so we'll put Mac's bowls away. He doesn't need them—Mac is not coming back. We are sad and we'll miss him, but we'll be okay. Daddy will be here and Mama will be here and we love you." This seemed to satisfy Liam, for he nodded and toddled off to play.

But a few minutes later, he was tugging at his mother's legs again, pointing to the boxes. She knew that small children like and need to hear things repeated, especially something new and unfamiliar. So she got down on her knees and explained again. She was careful to use the same words, to avoid confusing Liam. Still, repeating that Mac had died and was never coming back was difficult for her; it made her feel sad and tearful. It's hard enough to talk about the death of one you love—and Mac was like a member of the family—let alone repeat it over and over. But she went through the explanation several more times for Liam, and each time he nodded and kissed her and seemed reassured. It made Ginny feel that she was doing the right thing. Maybe Liam was beginning to understand. But then he'd come back again.

Ginny went upstairs and discovered Mac's bed of pillows in the hallway outside Liam's room. That was where Mac always slept, as if he were guarding the baby. She took the pillows down to the garbage can, feeling choked up but also relieved to be rid of the old hairy things. Liam found her in the act of throwing Mac's bed out, and he started pointing and jabbering excitedly. Again she explained about death, holding Liam and comforting him. "Liam, honey, Mac is dead. He's not sick and he's not in pain anymore. But he's not coming back. When animals die they don't sleep, so Mac doesn't need his bed. Dying is not like sleeping. We're going to miss Mac, and we're sad now, but we'll be okay. Mommy and Daddy love you." Returning her hug, Liam nodded and ran off to play. But he was soon back once more, pointing to the bed in the garbage can.

After his mother explained again with the same words, Liam nodded solemnly, gave her a hug and a smile, and began to play with his trucks. Ginny went to find Mark. She told him that Liam was curious about Mac's dishes and bed being put away, and she described the explanations she was offering Liam.

"The next time he comes back—and I'm sure he'll be back— why don't you watch me explain. Then you can explain, too," she said. "He'll feel better if something this important comes from both parents. And I think it's easier to begin talking to him about death now, before he's old enough to ask hard questions. Before it's the death of a grandparent we have to explain."

Mark hesitated. Mac's death still upset him very much. It was difficult for both Ginny and Mark to accept the sudden, shocking absence of a life that had been such a positive, generous, loving part of the household. Nevertheless, he agreed to try. When Liam next returned to investigate the boxes and the bed, Mark did a good job of reassuring him.

With both his mom and his dad reminding him of his own safety and their love, and telling him the simplest facts about death, Liam quickly adjusted to life without Mac. He seemed to forget all about his beloved dog—until he would find a toy of Mac's in a corner or a half-chewed rawhide bone hidden under the couch. Liam would bring Mac's possession to his mother or father, talking excitedly in his own language. They would repeat what they had already said, sometimes adding to it a little.

"Liam, everything that lives will die. Flowers die, trees and leaves die, animals die, and people die, too. When things die they don't move. They don't breathe. They don't eat. They don't sleep. Their lives stop, and they go back to being part of the earth so new things can live and grow—it's the circle of life."

Liam probably didn't understand everything his parents said, but his knowledge grew as he grew. His parents wanted death to be familiar to him, not to come as a total, frightening shock. The family knew many young children who had no information about death, who had no way to cope with the loss and confusion it could create in their lives. Liam's parents wanted him to know the simple facts of death so he would be able to ask his own questions and seek reassurance from those who loved him.

When Liam was two, he became fascinated with insects. He would squash them under his shoe and then poke the dead bodies with a stick, staring intently to detect any lingering movement. When the next live insect came along—stomp! Then he'd test that one with a stick. Over and over again, Liam performed his experiments. At first they seemed unnecessarily cruel, but as his mother watched, she realized that Liam was exploring what it meant to be "dead." When she asked what he was doing, he said with newly acquired words, "Move again? Come back like TV? This one die too when I stomp it?"

Repetition is the way we all learn, young children especially. They try something out, observe the results, make an assumption about the experience, then test it again. All the children at Liam's preschool were absorbed by similar experiments with insects. Other deaths came into the children's world, too. A dead robin was found in the preschool backyard, a dead fish floated in the fish tank, and a dead mouse was found in the preschool cellar. All were gleefully held between little fingers, while parents and teachers cringed. The bodies were carefully stroked, gently pinched, checked for breathing or other signs of life, then passed around with reverence and awe.

If the animal was one of the preschool pets that the children had cared for, their teachers helped the children hold a little funeral ceremony. The teachers explained that when an animal or a person dies, the organs inside—the brain, heart, lungs, stomach, liver, intestines—stop working. Because the body is no longer alive and healthy, with its own natural defenses, bacteria cause it to decompose, or rot. This creates a terrible smell. If left out in the open air, the body can become a good place for a number of diseases to grow. So, for the health of the living, it is important to bury a dead body or decompose it through cremation.

The children's pet funerals usually involved digging a hole in the preschool garden, then gently putting their small friend in it. They scooped dirt back into the hole and sprinkled flower seeds over it. The children took turns saying what they liked or remembered about their pet. "Tommy, the turtle, always ate his lettuce and never ran away." "Angel, the angelfish, was very beautiful and never ate the other fish." Then they would sing a good-bye song, holding hands. "Good-bye, Tommy . . . Good-bye, Tommy . . . Good-bye, Tommy . . . We're sad to see you go . . ." This was often followed by a chorus of "Inch by inch, row by row . . . Going to watch this garden grow . . ." As they added the flower seeds to the grave, they completed the cycle of life to death to life. Field mice and other dead creatures were also added to the garden to help the flowers grow, but without a ceremony. In this way, Liam and his friends came to understand that death and life are closely connected.

One two-year-old girl, whom Liam's family knew, was very disturbed by the sudden heart attack and death of her grandmother. Repeatedly she asked her mother, "Where's Nana? Where's Nana?" Her mother did her best to explain about death and cremation. But the grandmother's cremains were not yet buried in the cemetery, so there was nowhere to take the girl to visit.

The girl's mother found it very upsetting to have to repeat the story of Nana's death over and over for her young daughter. She herself felt sad and full of grief. She wanted to go off alone to cry, to remember, to mourn. "Each time my daughter asks that question, I feel like a knife is turning in my stomach," she told Liam's mother. Finally, when asked for the hundredth time, "Where's Nana? Where's Nana?" the child's mother took Nana's cremains and dumped them into an empty sand table. "There's Nana!" she said in desperation. "That's all that is left of her body now." The little girl gently sifted the pebblelike bits of bone through both hands. She smiled and murmured, "Play with Nana! Play with Nana!" She seemed to accept the surprising answer with calm satisfaction. Her fingers and skin gave her an understanding that her young mind could not formulate from words alone.

But, for the most part, it was the death of pets Liam and his friends were concerned with. If the children were allowed to satisfy their natural curiosity, if the surrounding adults answered questions openly and willingly, the deaths of animals were neither frightening nor confusing. There was trouble only when adults tried to ignore the deaths or be less than honest about them.

Liam's mother heard of such trouble at another preschool, where the children were three, four, and five years old. One day the teachers were occupied with an electric popcorn popper that was smoking. While they had their backs turned, some of the kids opened the guinea pig's cage and took Blackie out. They knew they weren't supposed to take him out of his cage without adult supervision, so, after playing with him for a minute or so, they panicked and tried to hide him. They pushed Blackie deep into the sand table, heaping sand over him until he was completely covered.

After a few minutes, the teachers turned around and noticed that the children were behaving strangely. No one would say what was wrong, and a short while passed before the teachers discovered that Blackie was missing. The children looked guilty, hiding their hands behind their backs, keeping their eyes downcast. They claimed they didn't know where their guinea pig was. One little girl volunteered that a bad man had stolen Blackie. Finally the preschoolers pointed to the sand table. Blackie was found—but he was no longer breathing. In the time it had taken to locate him, he had suffocated under the sand and was dead.

The horrified teachers quickly helped the children hold a little funeral for Blackie. They lifted him into a box. Each child said good-bye to him, stroking his fur and adding a special stone to the box. Then the teachers closed the lid. The children took turns digging a hole in the garden, put the box into it, and filled the hole with dirt. After that they sang, "Good-bye, Blackie . . . Good-bye, Blackie . . . Good-bye, Blackie . . . We're sad to see you go . . ." and planted flower seeds. The teachers talked about the cycle of life and death, explaining that Blackie's body would slowly decompose and turn into good rich soil that would help the flowers grow. It was a satisfying ceremony and the children liked participating. But no one ever talked about *why* Blackie had died.

The next day when the children arrived at preschool, there was a new guinea pig in the cage. It had shiny dark fur just like Blackie's. Many of the children were confused: It wasn't Blackie—or was it? Others were angry; did the teachers think they could pretend this guinea pig was as good as Blackie? Some of the children even tried to hurt the new guinea pig—called Shadow—poking it with pencils and scissors whenever the teachers weren't looking. Two weeks went by. Still the children did not like Shadow and often tried to hurt him.

Finally, the desperate preschool teachers called a counselor for advice. "We've created twelve little homicidal maniacs! Help! We don't know what to do. We told their parents how Blackie died, but should we tell them that their kids are trying to kill the new guinea pig, too? What has happened?"

After the counselor had listened to the whole story, she asked the teachers if they had ever talked with the children about *why* Blackie had died. "Oh, no! We couldn't do that." The counselor asked them why not. One teacher said, "Because the children killed him!" And the other cried, "Because I wasn't paying attention!" The counselor understood that the teachers felt as angry, guilty, and confused as the children. Once the teachers spoke their feelings out loud, they realized it, too.

"Blackie died because he got sand in his lungs and could no longer breathe," the counselor began gently. "Your children didn't mean to kill him. There was no intention to harm Blackie. Of course, they shouldn't have taken him out of the cage without supervision. They knew that was a rule. They need to understand that there was a good reason for the rule and that breaking it is where their responsibility lies. Now they're trying to hurt this new guinea pig to clear up the mystery about what makes something die, and also because they're angry about being asked to let Shadow replace Blackie. And they're scared. They feel they've done something wrong, but the consequences of their action haven't been clearly explained to them. It's too soon for them to love another guinea pig, especially when they feel confused and guilty about Blackie's death. First they have to understand what happened. Then they have to grieve and let go of their feelings about Blackie.

"Tell them that living things need air to breathe and that there is no air under sand. That's why Blackie died. Tell them that this is one reason adults don't want kids to play around construction sites where there are big piles of dirt and sand—because they might get buried and not be able to breathe, and then they would die, too. That's what the children need to know. Tell them these facts. And then tell them about your own feelings and invite the children to air theirs. But keep facts and feelings separate. First everyone needs to understand what happened. Then explore how it makes everyone feel. After that you can forgive one another and heal from this upsetting experience."

The counselor suggested some questions the teachers might begin with. Bearing these in mind, the teachers went back to the preschool and had a talk about Blackie. "Children, come sit in a circle. As you all know, two weeks ago our dear guinea pig, Blackie, died. Why do you think he died?" The teachers were surprised to hear one girl say, "Because I didn't clean my toys up and I was bad all day!" Another child answered, " 'Cause we wanted popcorn and it burned." A third declared, "Because we were bad and killed him!" The teachers told the children the real reason for Blackie's death, as they had rehearsed it with the counselor. The kids nodded solemnly. They accepted their responsibility for breaking the rule and not speaking up sooner about where Blackie was. But they were relieved to hear they were not murderers and bad people as they had feared. They never meant to hurt Blackie.

When the teachers asked the children how they felt about Shadow, they said they didn't really want a new guinea pig. They asked the teachers to take Shadow away. The teachers realized it was a mistake to try to keep them from feeling sad and upset by replacing the lost pet so soon. The children's reaction showed the teachers that it was better for the preschoolers to experience missing Blackie and being sad about his death. They should not be asked to pretend their grief didn't exist. The children knew they had feelings and only needed the space and encouragement to feel them and then go on. Three months later, the children decided they were ready for a new guinea pig. But this time they chose one that was a different color than Blackie.

When Liam was three he began to ask questions about Mac. He would look at his baby pictures, which often included Mac, and ask, "Who's that dog?" Liam's parents told stories of how Mac had licked him from head to toe when he came home from the hospital, and how Mac could run and jump higher than Daddy's head to catch a Frisbee. And they told him that Mac had died before Liam could talk. He listened attentively, repeated the stories back to his parents, and looked at the pictures often. One day his aunt's dog, Otto, died during an operation to fix his leg. Liam took the news philosophically. "Mac was black. And Otto was black. Do all black things die?" he asked.

"Well, all living things die. And sometimes living things are black, like Mac and Otto. But Mac and Otto didn't die because they were black. They died because they were sick and couldn't get well again. They won't come back now that they are dead. There is nothing we can do to change that."

Liam was struggling, as all children do, to understand the hardest fact about life: that individual lives come to an end. And he was doing a better job of it than many adults. He was not afraid to ask questions and to explore what was difficult for him to understand. His parents were careful not to transfer their learned fears and sadness about death onto Liam, so he could be free to have his own experiences and feelings.

How Liam dealt with the death of Mac, and how this loss was treated by his parents, gave Liam a way of coping that he would repeat and build upon when other losses occurred in the future. Even though he couldn't speak at the time, Liam was reassured by hearing the facts about death while receiving the affection of life. This knowledge and love gave him the ability to be comfortable with what he could not fully understand.

When Liam was four, he asked his mother, "What is a spirit?" Ginny sighed, feeling momentarily overwhelmed by the thought of explaining such a complex mystery. After all, did she know herself what a spirit is? Then she thought of a hand game that might help. She held one hand up in the air and wiggled it. "You see, Liam, some people believe that before you were born you were a spirit living up in heaven or in the universe. Pretend your spirit was this hand. And when you were born, your spirit slipped into your body, like a hand slipping into a glove." Ginny joined her two hands together, palms flat, and moved them simultaneously. "While you are alive, you go through life with your spirit inside your body, like a hand inside a glove. But when it is time to die, the body lies down and the spirit slips out and returns to the universe or heaven. And the body is left on earth, empty like an old glove."

Liam tried wiggling his own hands, together and then separately. He still looked puzzled. Ginny admitted to him that it was a hard thing to understand, and they would try again when he was five or six.

Liam was much better at understanding cemeteries. He took great pleasure in driving past the rows of white stone markers that lined the hillsides. He would always sing out, *"That's* a cemetery! *That's* where they put people in the ground. *Dead* people!" He enjoyed the power his knowledge gave him over a great mystery, and he was proud of his understanding.

■ CREATIVE SURVIVAL STRATEGIES

Take a walk outside and touch different things like grass, rocks, leaves, sticks, bugs! Is it alive or dead? Was it ever alive? How can you tell? Have you ever touched a dead animal? How did it feel? The next time you find one—touch it! Death is not dirty. There may be bacteria on the animal, but you can wash your hands well later with soap and hot water. Your eyes and fingers can help you understand what is hard to understand only in words. Does it scare you? Get some hugs!

If you have a pet that you love and it dies, you might want to arrange a funeral for it. You probably have some ideas yourself. Is there a special place the body should go? Can you help dig the hole? How do you want to say good-bye, since you won't see your pet again? Is there something you want to put in the hole with it that is especially from you? Is there a way you want to mark the grave, with rocks or a sign or something else? Plant a favorite flower or vegetable there so that your pet's death can help make new life grow. How about singing a special song or making some music to say good-bye? The simple beat of a drum, over and over, is the way some Native American Indians say good-bye to their dead ones. Can you remember a time you and your pet did something together that made you happy? Tell a story about it. And you can say how you feel right now, too. It's good to do this ceremony with someone that you love and trust, who can give you hugs if you feel sad or scared.

Try to use all your senses in your ceremony. *Touch* your pet "good-bye," *smell* the air and plants around you, *listen* to the songs and stories, *look* at the special place and remember it. And when you are done, *taste* something good to drink or eat. Your senses will help you feel better about the death and understand that it is part of life. You can take a deep breath and feel all your senses tingle with the sights, smells, sounds, tastes, and feelings of being alive.

■ FURTHER EXPLORATIONS

There is a wonderful book about a little boy and the death of his cat, Barney. *The Tenth Good Thing About Barney*, by Judith Viorst, is the story of the cat's funeral and the boy's feelings and efforts to understand what happens after someone we love dies.

Where the Red Fern Grows, by Wilson Rawls, is an adventure story of a boy who walks miles to bring home two puppies, raising them until they grow into his best friends. When death comes into their lives, we learn that animals as well as people grieve the loss of their loved ones.

Erik & Grammy

Death of a Grandparent

When Erik was six years old, his family moved into a big old house with lots of rooms. In the middle of the night, Erik heard noises that sounded as if people were walking back and forth through the house. The noises came from the wooden floorboards of his bedroom, but Erik thought there were ghosts around. He had nightmares about them and refused to sleep in his room alone. Erik's parents explained that the sounds came from the old floors, and after a few months Erik got used to his new home and its creaks and groans. His scary dreams went away, though he still preferred to have his older sister sleep in his room, too.

A year later, when Erik was seven, his grandmother became very sick from recurring breast cancer. Three years before, when Erik was four, she had been hospitalized to surgically remove her breast, a process called mastectomy. Then she was given chemotherapy treatments. The chemotherapy medicine was powerful enough to kill the cancer cells inside her body, but it also killed many healthy cells. This caused her hair to fall out and made her vomit. After the chemotherapy treatments were over, his grandmother felt better. Her hair grew back, and she was able to go home and take care of herself.

But this time chemotherapy did not help. Erik's grandmother did not regain her strength. She was too weak to live alone in her own house, so she came to live with Erik's family. Within a few weeks, Erik's parents knew that Grammy would soon die. She could hardly eat or drink anything. Her mouth was so full of sores from the chemotherapy, she had to be fed soft yogurt or pudding with a rubber baby spoon. Erik would sometimes help Grammy drink by squeezing water into her mouth with an eyedropper. And sometimes, through her thin nightgown, he could see the red scar on her chest where her breast used to be.

The doctor said there was nothing more he could do to make Grammy well. The cancer was too advanced—it had spread from her breasts to her lymph glands and other organs in her body. He could just give her medication for pain, to make her as comfortable as possible, and ask hospice workers to come help Erik's family take care of her. A hospice is a program run by a team of nurses, doctors, counselors, and volunteers who help give special care to dying people either in their homes or in a hospital. They give assistance, information, and comfort to family members as well.

Erik's family wanted to give Grammy special care at home, so she would not die alone in the hospital. But they worried that Erik's frightening dreams would return when Grammy died in their house. So they asked the hospice counselor to help Erik deal with his fears and nightmares.

When the hospice counselor knocked on the door for the first time, Erik's father opened it quickly. "Did the nurse send you?" he asked, with a frightened look on his face and panic in his voice.

"Ah, yes . . . she spoke to me last week. And I phoned you —I'm the hospice counselor. I'm here to work with Erik."

"Oh. *Oh!* We just called the nurse and asked her to send someone now because we think she's just *gone!* Shh . . . Erik doesn't know!" He pointed to a bed in the adjacent living room, then pulled a small scared-looking boy from behind him. "Here, sit at the table right here!" He urged Erik toward the counselor.

Erik and the counselor sat down at the dining-room table, near the front door. The counselor smiled and said hello to Erik, then pulled out colored markers and paper. On the other side of the living room, which adjoined the dining room, there was a bed with a body in it. A sheet had been pulled up, leaving only a bald head and a thin old face exposed. Erik glanced at the bed across the room, then at the counselor, and quickly began to draw trucks.

While the counselor thought about how to proceed, she started to draw a picture of Erik. She had just completed his head and neck when Erik took the paper and said excitedly, "That looks like my grammy! See, all her hair fell out because she's so sick!" Then he drew little wispy hairs on the head. "That's all she has left!"

Together they turned the drawing into a picture of Grammy, adding the collar of her lace nightgown and giving her big eyes and a smile. As they drew, Erik told the counselor about some of the things he and Grammy had done together. Before his family had moved into this big old house, his mother and father and sisters had lived across town in an apartment in Grammy's house. She had cooked spaghetti and had told Eric stories about her childhood way back when ice-cream cones cost only a nickel. Eric talked about the move and how he used to think there were ghosts in his house. He didn't look too certain that they had gone away for good.

Kelly, one of Eric's sisters, came by and asked if the nurse had arrived. She knew that her grandmother was dead and that the hospice nurse would come and check Grammy's body to verify the death. Then the nurse would notify the doctor and arrange for the funeral director to come and remove the body. Kelly sat down at the table. The counselor knew Erik needed to be told that his grandmother had died, even though he probably sensed it from his father's nervousness and what he had seen and overheard.

The counselor didn't feel she could tell Erik. The news should come from someone he knew and trusted, not from someone he had never met before. But his parents were not in the room. If Erik wasn't told soon, he would find out when the nurse, priest, and funeral director walked through the door, and that would be a terrible shock and make him feel excluded.

As they drew more pictures, the counselor said to Erik's sister, "Kelly, Erik doesn't know about Grammy."

Kelly looked surprised. "Oh! Grammy's dead, Erik! Do you wanna see her?"

Erik's eyes grew round and fearful, but he nodded. So the three of them got up from the table and went over to the bed.

Grammy was so thin she seemed almost like a skeleton. Her waxy-looking skin was almost transparent. Her mouth sagged a little but was utterly still. Her arms were stretched out by her sides, palms up, as though she was waiting for something. Grammy looked very peaceful, very quiet—and, to the hospice counselor, very dead.

But to seven-year-old Erik, she may have looked only asleep.

The counselor gently touched Grammy's body and found her arm to be cool though her neck was still warm. Slowly the body was assuming the temperature of the room, now that it was no longer heated from within by a heart that pumped and lungs that breathed. The hospice counselor could also see red splotches forming on the skin under Grammy's shoulders and neck. Gravity was pulling the blood down to the underside of the body, where it formed interior pools that showed up as splotches. The counselor told Erik he could touch Grammy if he wanted to. Erik shook his head no and quickly put his hands behind his back. He looked scared. The counselor asked him if he wanted to draw again. He nodded silently and bolted back to the table in the dining room.

This time Erik drew airplanes fighting each other in the sky and crashing into the ocean.

"What happens to the pilots when the planes crash in the water?" the counselor asked.

"They die!" Erik answered, firmly.

"What happens when they die? Do they still eat when they die?"

"No. . . . They don't eat anymore. You don't eat when you're dead," Erik replied, very sure of this fact.

"Do the pilots still breathe after they are dead?" the counselor asked.

"No." This time Erik hesitated. "They don't breathe anymore. You don't breathe when you're dead."

"Right! The dead don't eat or breathe," the counselor agreed. "But are they sleeping? Do dead people sleep?"

"Yes! They are sleeping!" Eric declared.

The counselor knew that Eric might be confused about the difference between sleeping and death. He was only seven years old, and he had already been troubled by ghost dreams. Children often fear going to sleep after someone in their family dies. They are afraid that they too will keep on sleeping and never wake up.

It is a natural association. Many people, many cultures, have thought of death as a "final sleep."

So the counselor explained gently, "No, Erik. When you go to sleep, you always wake up. You go to sleep at night . . . then you wake up in the morning. Then you go to sleep the next night . . . and you wake up the next morning. Sleep . . . wake up . . . sleep . . . wake up. But when people die they are not asleep. They will not wake up. They are dead and gone and will not wake up again."

Erik nodded doubtfully. He did not quite believe this.

The counselor knew it would help Erik if he could understand death through his own senses. If he could touch his grammy, the incredible stillness of her body would tell him clearly that this was not sleep. But he had said he did not want to touch her. Urging or forcing him would do more harm than good.

At that point the nurse arrived, and Erik's family let her in. Erik watched from the table as the nurse listened for Grammy's heartbeat with a stethoscope. She told the assembled family that Grammy's heart had definitely stopped beating and that she had indeed died. The nurse left her stethoscope on the table as she and Erik's parents went into the kitchen. They would phone the funeral director and then the doctor, who would sign an official death certificate.

The counselor picked up the stethoscope and asked Eric if he had ever listened to his own heart. He shook his head and reached for the stethoscope eagerly. He put the ends into his ears and the round microphone over his heart. His eyebrows jumped as he suddenly heard the *thump-thump-thump* of his own heart. Erik listened with great concentration for a few minutes.

Then the counselor asked him if he wanted to listen to his sister's heart. Erik was curious to see what her heart sounded like. As Kelly's heart went *thhump—thhump—thhump*, Eric's eyebrows went up and down in rhythm. The counselor explained that since Kelly was seven years older than Erik, her heart beat much more slowly than his own. A baby's heart beats very fast, about 140 beats per minute, and then, as the baby grows into a child and then an adolescent and then an adult, the heart gradually slows. An adult's heart beats about sixty to eighty times per minute. Erik decided to try the stethoscope on the counselor. He turned to her as though he were a doctor doing a checkup. "May I listen to your heart, ma'am?" Erik confirmed that her heartbeat was indeed slower than Kelly's.

The counselor asked Eric what he thought Grammy's heart would sound like. He paused. Then he announced, "I don't know, but I'm going to find out." He marched over to her bed and placed the stethoscope on her chest, listening. Not finding a heartbeat there, he moved the microphone to the tip of her head and listened. Slowly he listened his way down her body until he reached her toes. Finally he turned around, took the stethoscope out of his ears, rested it on his neck, and said, "Nope! No heart beating! She's dead!"

Erik's pride in his new knowledge, which had come through

his fingertips and his ears, was obvious. His relief was clear, too. His senses had helped him understand something important about what death was. His hearing and sense of touch had shown him what his mind alone could not grasp.

A few days later, Erik said to his mother, "I know where Grammy's heart is. . . . It's inside my heart!" Listening to his own heartbeat and then listening to his grandmother's stilled heart had helped Erik make a connection between living and dying. It had allowed him to formulate his feeling that the love between him and his grandmother could live on inside of him, even though she was gone. After her death, Erik was rarely bothered by dreams about ghosts again.

What Erik showed his family was that words are not enough to understand the reality of dying—not for a seven-year-old, and not for anyone, really. To see the immovable face of death, to touch the absolute stillness of a body, to hear no heartbeat—these sensory experiences give all of us concrete knowledge of death. This knowledge helps ease our fears of death, fears that may be instilled by others or played upon by television and movies, or that may simply be the result of our ignorance and inexperience. Years ago, when it was common for extended families of different generations to live together, everyone had more firsthand knowledge of death.

At the same time, direct sensory experience of a death can sometimes be frightening. It helps to have a medium or bridge, as the stethoscope was for Erik. Japanese families achieve this bridge through a Shinto ceremony, a hands-on ritual, at death. Everyone, including children, washes and anoints the dead person's body with oil, then helps wrap it in beautiful silks. Participation in such rites should never be forced on anyone. But traditions and rituals can give a sense of mastery and order that enable us to conquer our fears. They make us feel we are an intimate and important part of the life and death that goes on around us all the time. In so doing, they help us fear our own deaths less.

■ CREATIVE SURVIVAL STRATEGIES

Borrow a stethoscope from a nurse or doctor and find your own heartbeat. Then listen to someone else's. . . . Is it different? Besides listening for a heartbeat, how else can you tell that someone is dead? Many years ago, people used to hold a mirror under a person's nose. If it fogged over it meant that the person was still breathing, still alive. The human breath carries moisture that condenses into fog when it comes into contact with a cool mirror. It's also possible to test for death by lifting a person's eyelid to see if the dark inner pupil is very large, or dilated. If a flashlight is shone into the eye and the pupil doesn't contract (get small) when the bright light hits it, that's a sign the person is dead. Doctors describe this condition by saying "the pupils are fixed and dilated." Have you ever heard of an EEG, or electroencephalograph? This is a machine with small metal disks and wires that can be attached to the head. Those metal sensors measure the electrical activity in the brain and can tell us whether or not someone is "brain dead" even though their heart may still be beating. When this happens, the family may decide to let the person die by stopping treatments that are keeping the heart beating, such as the use of a respirator that pumps air into the lungs. This is also the time when organs from the brain-dead person may be surgically removed from the body and donated to others who desperately need a new heart or lung to live.

Try drawing a ghost story of your own. What is happening in your story? Is someone dead? Does that person come back to Earth as a ghost? Do you know of religions that believe in spirits or ghosts? How are those beliefs different from the horror movies made in Hollywood? Can bodies really rise out of graves and come back to haunt the living? Do these Hollywood movies make you feel afraid to go to a cemetery to pay your respects to a dead loved one? How can you tell the difference between fantasy and reality? Discuss these issues with adults in your family, or with teachers or people at your church. Find out what ghost stories they used to hear when they were kids and how they feel about cemeteries now.

What do you think happens to people when they die? Some religions believe that each person has a spirit or soul that lives on eternally in a nonphysical form in heaven. And some religions believe that a person's soul is reborn or reincarnated into a new form, such as an animal, insect, or human being. What explanations of death make sense to you and your family?

■ FURTHER EXPLORATIONS

There is a very sensitive book about the special relationship between grandparents and a grandchild, called *Blackberries in the Dark*, by Mavis Jukes. It tells the story of a nine-year-old boy's first extended visit to his grandparents' house after the death of his grandfather, where he explores his grief and finds acceptance of his loss.

Lori & Barry

Death of a Father

Lori stood on the top step, looking down the carpeted stairs into the family room. More people. This time it was the visiting nurse, the equipment man, her mom, the neighbors, and someone from her father's office. They were all gathered around her dad in his new hospital bed, talking loud and laughing about the big effort it had taken to get the bed down the stairs of the split-level house. Lori's dad needed the bed—badly. He was so weak he needed the bed's electric lift to raise him up to sit. He was so thin he needed its soft water-bed mattress with a pump attached to circulate the water and alter the pressure under his body. His regular mattress had rubbed sores into his skin.

Lori didn't go down—there probably wouldn't be room for her. And she didn't think this was anything to joke about . . . a hospital bed for her sick father. So she stayed on the top step, feeling anxious and left out.

Lori knew that animals died—she had seen that. When her neighbor's cat had been hit by a car, she had touched the white fur of the deathly still Snowball as it lay by the curb. And she knew that old people could die. Her grandmother had died three years ago. But she had lived in another state; Lori had never felt close to her. People whom Lori *knew* didn't die. Especially not someone like her dad. He used to be big and strong and laugh a lot. He had always taken Lori to Paragon Park and gone on all the terrifying rides with her; they had screamed together until their throats hurt. He was a young dad. And Lori was only eight—he couldn't die. Then why was he in that bed?

Ever since her dad had found a black mole on his back and the doctor had diagnosed it as a skin cancer called melanoma, he had been sick from radiation treatments. He had had to lie strapped to a table while a giant X-ray machine shot invisible rays into the cancer cells to try to kill them. The treatments burned his skin and made his stomach hurt. They also made his big bushy mustache, which used to smell like tobacco and shaving cream, fall out. All of his hair had fallen out, too, leaving pink skin stretched tightly over a smooth skull. The radiation treatments that were supposed to make him better had just made him bald, so far as Lori could see.

Lori's mother had explained that the cancer cells had traveled from his back, where they had started growing, through his body to his liver. The cancer cells grew very fast there, creating a lump, or tumor, that pressed on the liver and made it swell. The liver, which was surrounded by tissue that gave it its own place in the body, wasn't meant to increase in size. Its enlargement caused great pain for her father. He hardly smiled now. He was too weak to go to the office or on business trips or to the Little League games he used to coach. He didn't even come to the supper table anymore. Lori's mother brought him meals on a tray. But when the tray came back, it looked to Lori as though her father had just poked his food around, not eaten any. No wonder he was so weak he couldn't sit up without help. Lori's mom had to lean over so he could wrap his arms around her shoulders. Then she'd straighten up, and he'd be able to rise to a sitting position. But now the hospital bed would take care of that.

There were always a lot of people around, too. Like today. Hospice nurses and their assistants who took care of Lori's father; friends, neighbors, and people from work who kept stopping by to visit. It was hard to get time alone with him. Why were all these people here? Couldn't they leave him be and let him get well? He just got worse, not better. But he couldn't die, could he?

Lori kept this terrifying question to herself. She didn't ask her mother or tell her brothers—Eric, sixteen, or Barry, twelve—about her fear. It was too scary to say, "Is my daddy going to die?" She was afraid that asking something like that would make it really happen. She didn't even want to think about it, but the worry and the words kept coming into her mind. Especially at school. She found it hard to pay attention. The teacher would scold her, and then Lori would get mad and yell back. For the first time ever, she began to be sent to the principal's office.

Even at home, it seemed she was always saying the wrong thing, stupid things that she didn't mean—telling her mom that she was a witch for not letting her go to her friend's house on a school night or for making a dinner Lori didn't like. Then Lori would have a tantrum—yell at them all, slam doors. Afterward she'd be sent to her room and have to sit there all alone. She never used to act this way. Is something wrong with me? Lori worried. But she was scared of that question, too.

As the trouble with Lori continued over the weeks, her mother knew it must have something to do with Lori's dad. Since she didn't know how to help, she asked the social worker from the hospice to come and talk to Lori. The hospice had provided the new hospital bed. The hospice nurses brought over medicine and worked hard to find ways to keep Lori's dad as comfortable and free of pain as possible.

When the hospice social worker made her regular visits to

Lori's mom and dad, Lori was usually in school. After Lori's mom explained about the trouble Lori was having, the social worker agreed to come later in the day and meet with her. She introduced herself to Lori and took out a new box of crayons, asking if Lori would like to draw with her. Lori was suspicious but also interested.

"What should I draw?" she asked.

"How about a picture of your dad?" the social worker suggested. "I know he's very sick with cancer and being taken care of right here in your house."

So Lori drew a picture of her father in the hospital bed. She included the mattress filled with water that kept his back from getting sore. And she added a big metal triangle that hung over his head. For a short time, her dad had been able to pull himself up with it. When asked about this big black "trapeze," Lori said, "I hate that thing! Every time I lean over the bed and try to kiss him, it hits me on the head!" Since her dad was too weak to use it anymore, the social worker suggested they simply remove it. Now it just got in the way of the family being close. Lori was pleased with this idea.

The social worker pointed to Lori's drawing and asked about the dark marks on top of her dad's head. "Oh!" said Lori. "He doesn't have any hair now—the radiation made his hair fall out."

Then the social worker pointed to the odd-shaped yellow feet Lori had given him.

"See, he keeps getting skinnier and skinnier on his body here," Lori explained. "But his feet keep getting fatter and fatter, and I'm afraid one day they might pop like a balloon!"

Her dad's feet were swollen because his liver was pressing on the blood vessels that went to his legs. This pressure prevented fluids like blood and lymph from circulating properly, so the fluids pooled in his feet. Also, because Lori's dad could eat very little, the chemical balance in his cells was upset. The cells were no longer able to move the fluids they produced out and into the bloodstream. So the tissues swelled.

"I can see why his feet would scare you; they do look like balloons," said the social worker. "But feet have much thicker skins than balloons, and your dad's are not going to pop. We can put some extra pillows under them to prop them up. That way

Lori's drawing of her dad in a hospital bed, and her attempts to help him.

gravity will pull the fluids down into his legs and reduce the swelling a little."

Lori looked relieved and was ready to draw again. "What now?" she asked.

"Well, what about you, Lori? If you were in this picture, what would you be doing?"

Lori immediately began to draw. "This is me bringing tea to my daddy."

"Do you help take care of your daddy, bring him tea and things?" The social worker was impressed.

"Oh, no!" said Lori. "He's too sick! He's so sick that the family room door is closed almost all the time while people are with him. I can't hardly see him anymore, and I don't know what's going on in there!"

Clearly, Lori wanted to help her father, but she felt shut out of his care. So the social worker took the drawing to Lori's mother to show her what Lori needed.

Lori's mother had been upset by how her husband's appearance had changed since the melanoma had spread to his liver. His face was yellow and thin, while his abdomen was so swollen that he didn't look like the same man. She was worried that his distorted body would frighten Lori, and her mother wanted to protect her.

The social worker explained that Lori's fears were probably worse than her father's real condition, no matter how bad he might look. We can often imagine much more horrifying scenes than those that life presents to us. And it hurts us and scares us to be left out. But if we can help take care of someone we love —even someone weak, in pain, and disfigured—our feelings of love make us strong. They soften the harsh reality of serious illness and lessen our fears.

Lori's mom agreed to keep the door open as much as possible so that all the kids could feel free to wander in and out for quick hellos. Each day Lori and her older brothers could also have private visits with their dad. During those times they could talk together, read, watch TV, or do whatever they wanted. Because Lori had been able to show her fears and wishes in her drawing, she was able to receive the reassurance and help she needed.

But Lori's drawing revealed even more. The social worker shared the drawing with the hospice artist. The artist noticed that although Lori had drawn herself helping, she had not given herself any hands. That's how helpless Lori was feeling. Once Lori knew what to do and was allowed to help, she had fewer temper tantrums at home, and there were hardly any more violent outbursts at school. Lori still felt angry many times, but mostly she was very sad. Sometimes her tears overflowed in the classroom. Her teacher understood and let Lori go home, where she felt better being with her father. He recognized that Lori's sadness and tears were grief for him, and he hugged Lori as tightly as he could.

Two months later, Lori's dad was no longer able to be helped out of bed. His throat was so swollen he could eat only soft food like ice cream. There were small tumors all over his chest that looked like marbles pressing up through his skin. Some of them bled and had to be bandaged. The odor of dried blood mingled with the smells of alcohol and air freshener in his room.

Lori's dad needed more medicine each day to control the pain caused by the pressure his enlarged liver exerted on his other organs. His whole abdominal area was so swollen he looked pregnant with his own death. The medicines made him drowsy, so he slept a great deal. Sometimes he didn't speak for a day or two, and then when he did, his whispered words often made no sense.

Lori's mother knew he would die soon. But Lori still had not been told that her dad would never get better. "She's only eight. . . . What should I say? Will she understand?" her mother worried. Yet Lori could see that her dad was getting worse every day.

The hospice team discussed how to help the family come to grips with this dilemma. The hospice artist had been working with Lori ever since she had shown such an interest in drawing with the social worker. Perhaps the hospice artist could find out what Lori believed was happening. Lori's mother thought Lori might talk more freely at the hospice office than at home, so she dropped Lori off one afternoon.

Lori and the artist sat down on the office floor amid paper and markers, and began to draw. Lori created a picture of her father surrounded by many, many hearts.

"Lori, it's so beautiful!" the hospice artist said. "So much love

Lori's drawing shows her love for her dad.

for your daddy—I can feel it! You must be feeling a lot of love for him to draw so many hearts—and then still more hearts in between those hearts!"

Lori gazed at her drawing with pride.

"But why is your dad so small?" the hospice artist asked.

Lori put her hands on her hips and looked a little disgusted. "Because he's *dying*, stupid!" she shouted.

The artist nodded in agreement and gave Lori a hug. The answer to the dilemma of what to tell Lori was right there in the drawing. Lori already knew what was happening. Her dad was shrinking out of her world, getting ready to walk out of his bed straight up to the sky, with a big smile because he had all of Lori's love to help him.

Lori already knew because she had heard people whispering, "Should we call your brother and tell him that it's time to come?" She had seen the worried faces of her family, seen the trays of uneaten food, watched her dad wither away before her. Lori could also see changes in the caregiving routines. Nurses came and stayed all night because her father was now too weak to call out when he needed help.

Lori sensed changes in the emotions of others. There was more tension, more crying, more silence whenever she entered the room. Lori knew death was coming. She just didn't know what it meant. She needed to be reassured that it was true: her father was dying, but her own life would go on. She needed to be told what changes her father's death would bring to her family and how these changes might feel. At his funeral, would she have to say a few words out loud? Who would come to the service? Would the relatives stay with them? When would she go back to school? Would the kids already know about her dad? Would her family have enough money in the future? Would they be able to continue living in the same house? Would her mom have to get a job? Would something terrible happen to her mom, too? What if she died also?

Her family could answer many of these questions but not, of course, all of them. No one knows exactly what the future will be. But Lori's mom sat down with Lori and her brothers to figure out what they could about their new routines. It was a relief to

begin to talk about these practical matters, because it turned their
minds, for a while, to a future beyond their father's suffering.
Planning was something they could do for one another when there
was nothing more they could do for him.

Lori's brother, Barry, was twelve years old and preparing for his
bar mitzvah when the mole on his dad's back was diagnosed as
melanoma. Getting ready for a bar mitzvah, a ceremony in Judaism
that marks a young man's coming-of-age, usually takes two years
of study and preparation. Barry's dad helped him pronounce Hebrew words and corrected Barry's recitation as much as he could,
but he grew tired easily. Barry knew it was traditional to turn
thirteen before having a bar mitzvah. But Barry's thirteenth birthday was half a year away, and he was worried that his dad would
die before then. His older brother, Eric, could help him a little
with his studying, but the ceremony wouldn't be the same without
his father. It was customary for a father to participate with the
son. Barry desperately wanted his dad to be there.

Barry's family talked the situation over with the hospice nurse,
who thought Barry's worry was well founded. So the family asked
the rabbi at their temple if it would be possible to perform the
bar mitzvah for Barry before he was thirteen. Could it be done
soon, in a few weeks? Permission was granted. On that great day,
Barry's father made his way down the aisle in a wheelchair.
Though extremely thin, he managed to stand and speak into the

microphone during the ceremony. He gazed at Barry proudly. As the family looked on, the two of them chanted, sang, and read Hebrew scripture. The entire event was tape-recorded.

Four weeks after Barry's bar mitzvah, his father died. Barry found comfort in listening to the tape of his father's voice reciting the Hebrew prayers of the ceremony. He felt very grateful to have shared his coming-of-age with his father, and very sad that it was the last experience they would share.

In the months that followed, Barry missed his father intensely. It was especially hard at his Little League games, because his dad had been the team's coach. Barry talked about these games at a Kids' Arts Group. This was a group where kids who had struggled with death in their families could get together to make projects and discuss common feelings and experiences. The hospice sponsored the group, which met every two weeks during the school year. Both Barry and Lori joined in the fall, two months after the death of their father.

At the first session, as a way of introducing themselves, all the kids were invited to bring objects that their deceased family members had given them. Lori brought a doll from Czechoslovakia, a banner from Holland, and a hat from Texas, all gifts her father had brought back to her from his travels. Barry came with his bat, glove, football, and baseball.

After they had all shared their stories and examined one another's treasures, they drew pictures and wrote about their gifts. Barry drew his bat and glove, and filled the space inside the drawings with these words:

> *My father has been my baseball coach for six years, that is,*
> *six GREAT YEARS. It was great having him for my baseball*
> *coach. He would always warm up the pitcher before the game*
> *started. Every time I was up to bat he gave me hand signals*
> *from third base on what I should do.*
>
> *Now when I look down at third base and see he is not*
> *there to give me hand signals, I say to myself before the*
> *pitch, "This one's for you Dad."*

Remembering the games filled Barry with a lonely sadness. But remembering them was better than remembering his dad sick, thin, and in pain. Making something from his memories of his father helped Barry feel closer to his dad, stronger in his love for him. In the same way, it helped him feel better to dedicate each one of his hits to his father, saying to himself, "This one's for you, Dad!"

We never get a choice about who will die in our lives. But we do get to choose what to do with our memories. By using our memories to make poetry, drawings, and stories, we create a truth we can live with. By turning our feelings of sadness, regret, loneliness, and anger into something we can touch, explore, and trea-

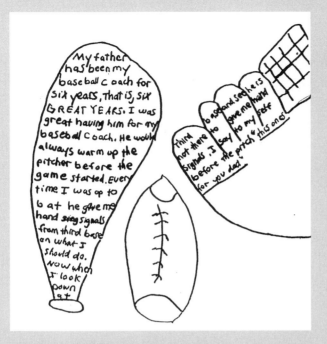

My father has been my baseball coach for six years, that is, six GREAT YEARS. I was great having him for my baseball coach. He would always warm up the pitcher before the game started. Every time I was up to bat he gave me hand signals from third base on what I should do. Now who I look down at

Third not there to give me hand signals. I say to my self before the pitch "this one for you dad."

Barry's baseball memories of his dad.

sure, we transform our grief so that it brings us new understanding, new strength.

As time goes by, as we grow, the meaning of a death changes. We change in our ability to understand what we have lost. Barry showed this in his drawing of a "broken heart." He filled the heart with these words, which he wrote after his thirteenth birthday.

Now that I've been through this tragic incident, it feels a lot different than before. Then I felt like it would never happen

*to me. I guess, unfortunately, that I was wrong. I feel now
like I want another chance to be with him, and one more
chance to say goodbye. Now since he is gone, my family
seems totally different. I miss my father telling me to go to
bed. For once in my life I would love to have him yell at
me. I really don't know why such bad things have to
happen to good people!!*

With these wrenching words, Barry grieved the loss of his father,
mourned the times together he knew would never come again.
He struggled to make sense of the injustice of losing his father
just when he needed him so much. To have one more connec-

Barry's drawing of his broken heart.

tion—a hug, a word, even in anger—would be so precious! When Barry turned these desperate feelings into a poem, it made him feel better. He was doing what people for thousands of years in every culture have learned to do with their feelings of grief: memorialize them in art. So much music, painting, sculpture, and writing has come from the pain of losing someone deeply loved. The art cannot replace what has been lost, nor does it make the loss worthwhile. But it can help us mourn by easing our pain and revealing the love we still carry.

■ CREATIVE SURVIVAL STRATEGIES

Make a taped audio or video recording of people in your family telling a favorite story, singing a song, or reading a book to you. Do this especially if you know someone in your family will die soon. Do you have any old home movies of your parents or grandparents or pets? Watch them! If you want to see them over and over, ask an adult to get them transferred to videotape so you can watch them alone safely.

Did someone who died give you a special gift that you want to treasure? Find it and draw a picture of it. Add a few words in the form of a poem about the gift and about your memories. Show your poem/drawing to your family and ask them what they remember about that person—things the person did or presents he or she gave to others in the family.

When Barry and Lori's father died, their family followed the Jewish mourning ritual of "sitting shivah." This tradition lasts for three to seven days after the funeral. Friends and family gather each evening to sit in a circle at the home, read Hebrew prayers, and tell stories about the deceased. Family members are usually not allowed to answer doors or phones or cook or wait on others, in recognition of their deep sorrow and their need to grieve and do nothing else. Instead, they listen to stories they may not have known about their loved one, enjoy memories of his or her life, and become used to the reality of the death. After shivah has ended, a rabbi might take the family outside for a walk around the neighborhood, to observe how much remains the same and how life goes on, despite the sadness and change brought by the loss. This tradition gives a family support after the funeral is over.

■ FURTHER EXPLORATIONS

When Barry was struggling to understand his father's dying, he read *Learning to Say Good-bye: When a Parent Dies,* by Eda LeShan. The book was written for adults, but it is helpful for children as well. Barry found it so valuable that he wrote to the author and thanked her. And he was thrilled when she wrote back to thank him for his letter and express her sadness at the loss of Barry's father.

David & His Mom

Death of a Mother

David sat staring at the piano keys; he just didn't have the energy to reach them. They seemed so far from his fingers. What did the music matter, anyway? He was only twelve years old and he knew his mother was dying.

Her cancer had started in her left eye and then spread to her bones. For almost a year she had been sick from the chemotherapy treatments. The strong medicine that was supposed to kill the cancer cells in her body had also killed many healthy cells. It made her dizzy and nauseous, and she threw up a lot. For the past two weeks, she hadn't come downstairs—not even to hear David play the piano, something she used to do every day despite her illness.

David played Mozart very well. He didn't make many mistakes, and he was proud of that. His mother would lie back in the recliner with her eyes closed, smiling. Her thin hands would wave in the air as though conducting. The music made her feel better, she said. For two weeks now, David had practiced alone every day, hoping the music would float up to her bedroom and make her happy.

Suddenly, he grew impatient with the piano. He slammed his hands down on the keys. It just wasn't the same without his mom. She should be down here, helping him keep the beat! He wandered into the kitchen and looked inside the refrigerator. But he wasn't really hungry. There were jars in the refrigerator, lots of jars, and bottles too. He took them all out and lined them up on the floor. Then he unscrewed the lids and began to blow gently across the glass openings. "Ooohh . . . oooohhhhh." The different jars and bottles made different hollow, windy tones. This could be music. Quickly David rearranged them in the order of the musical scale and tried blowing "The Star-Spangled Banner." It worked.

By the time the hospice nurse arrived to help take care of his mother, David was excited. "Hey! Listen to this!" he yelled. Blowing on jars of pickles, olives, and mayonnaise, he began to play the national anthem. The nurse, who was new, was surprised by what she saw on the floor. But she was also impressed. She ignored the mess and said, "You must be David. Has your mother heard this music?"

"No, she's too sick to come downstairs anymore," he answered, suddenly discouraged. But the hospice nurse wasn't discouraged. She helped David set up the jars on a tray and carry them up to his mother's room. There David performed his first "Refrigerator Concert." His mother loved it. She gently kept the beat, her hands waving in the air, and David felt happier than he had in a long while.

A month later, David's mother was so weak she could no longer talk, and this scared him. It was as though she wasn't there anymore. Yet she *was* there—her thin body was still breathing, and her hands would often flutter with movement as if a thought had run through them. She could still hear, and she was able to open and close her eyes to answer questions. One blink for "yes," two blinks for "no." But the sound of her voice—a sound David had known since before he was born—was missing. He knew she would soon be gone forever. He couldn't stand not being able to communicate with her while she was here with him. It was too terrifying to lose her while she was still alive.

David remembered a game he played at school called the Squeeze Game. He thought he could teach it to his mother. So he drew a "Squeeze Game Chart" and showed it to her, quietly explaining how the game was played. First, David squeezed his mother's hand four times, saying the four words "Do you love me?" Next, he told his mother to squeeze back three times for the three words "Yes, I do." She weakly closed her hand around his three times. Then David squeezed twice, saying "How much?" Then, together they both squeezed each other's hands tightly for a long time—to show they loved each other *that* much! He pointed to the bottom of the chart where he had written "I love you" and its symbolic code, "Eye (I) Heart (Love) Ewe (You)." She smiled, closed her eyes, and squeezed David's hand three times: "Yes, I do."

During the next three days, David sat by his mother's bed many times, telling her about his soccer games and events at school. But sometimes a quietness would steal over him. He would get a panicky feeling that she wasn't with him anymore, that he was

David's "Squeeze Game Chart."

losing her. He'd take her hand and call to her, saying "Mom . . . Mom . . . it's time to play the Squeeze Game."

Then David knew his mother was with him, listening, even if she couldn't talk. Her gentle squeezes told him she was still there, still loving him. And she knew that he loved her. When finally she could not return his touch, David understood that she was gone forever.

A few months after his mother's death, David began to attend the Kids' Arts support group. It was run by the hospice for children who had experienced a death in their family. At that time there were six children in the group. They engaged in many different activities—drawing, making up games, giving back rubs, and talking about what was changing in their lives because a person they loved had died.

One day David told everyone, "Last night the phone rang during dinner, and I got up to answer it. But when the man said, 'This is *The Boston Globe* calling. Is your mother there?' I froze! I couldn't talk! My father and brother and sister all started looking at me, and I was staring back at them. But I couldn't talk! I couldn't say my mother . . .'"

David couldn't say it to the group either: that his mother was *dead*. The paralyzing words made him feel ashamed and humiliated. It was horrible to be so different from everyone in his class and in his neighborhood. Everyone had a mother but David. What would happen when they had to make Mother's Day projects at school? Or when his mother was supposed to go to school for Parents' Day? What was wrong with him, that his mother should die and leave him so marked? Everyone who knew about it acted afraid of him or pretended it hadn't happened.

But when the other kids in the group started describing the same kinds of experiences, the same kinds of feelings, David began to relax. The kids decided to come up with a plan for what they would say on the phone the next time something like that happened. "I'm sorry, she can't come to the phone" was rejected as sounding weak and untruthful. But when they added, ". . . she can't come to the phone *because she's dead!*" they all liked that. It would sure get rid of a salesman! The idea of using the truth in a shocking way made the kids feel powerful despite a difficult situation. David smiled and practiced saying these words, role-playing with the others.

At another meeting of the Kids' Arts Group, the children started talking about not being able to remember what their parents or siblings had looked like when they were healthy, before they got sick. This clearly upset David. "I knew her twelve years and she was only sick one year!" he blurted out. "Why can't I remember? I must be stupid!" The images he saw of his mother in his dreams were also from when she was ill, lying in bed with her eyes closed. This was happening to the other children, too. So the group decided to do something about it. They created "Before and After" drawings of the family members they had lost.

In David's "After" drawing, every feature of his mother's face changed. Her big smile shrank to a small frown in a skinny face. Even her nose changed direction. Her hair went from wavy and full to limp and messy. But the biggest change was in her eyes. The left eye had a dark mark above it, and tears were flowing down that cheek. At the bottom of the paper under her picture, David added two drawings of himself—"because I changed, too," he said sadly.

The counselor who led the group told David that his drawing made her feel sad—sad that his mother had become so sick with cancer and sad that he suffered, too. He nodded in agreement. "What happened to your mother's eye?" she asked, pointing to the black mark.

David's drawings of his mom and himself before and after she got sick.

David sighed. "A long time ago, she got cancer in that eye, and they had to take it out. But she got a new glass eye, and it was a really good one. See? You couldn't tell it was a fake, could you?" He pointed to the eye in the "Before" drawing. "But this time when she got sick, she got so skinny that the skin around the glass eye pulled away, and you could see it wasn't real."

Everyone could tell that the false eye bothered David a lot, because he drew it often—floating on a mural the group painted, on the table-hockey score pad, or on random pieces of paper. Whenever he drew the eye, the kids all knew he was thinking about his mother. Then the counselor would ask him what had happened that day.

"I opened my lunch today—peanut butter and jelly, five days in a row! The same thing as yesterday, and every day," David said angrily. "My mother would never make me eat the same thing over and over!" Often it was some small but powerful reminder like this that told David his mother was gone and life would never be the same. And then David would draw the eye.

One day, David drew a picture of a face half covered by a giant baseball. He wrote on it "OW! My mother thought . . ." He quickly pushed the paper toward the counselor as if it were burning his fingers. She looked at it and told him it was a very scary drawing. The counselor also asked him what his mother thought.

"Well," he said hesitantly, "just before my mother died, she told me the reason she had to die was because when she was nine

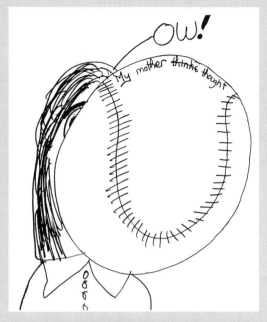

The story of David's mother's eye.

years old she got hit in the eye with a baseball. And that's why she got cancer and had to die!"

David was scared and shaking, so the counselor held him for a while. Then, without contradicting his mother, the counselor tried to explain why she might have said that. "David, for your mother to die and leave you was the hardest thing she ever had to do. And she wanted to give you a reason. But that doesn't mean that if you get hit with a baseball you will die! And it doesn't mean that things that hurt you now will come back and kill you later."

David relaxed a little, but still looked doubtful. So the counselor asked the others, "Has anyone got any scars? Did anyone ever break a bone?" And everyone started to roll up their sleeves and pant legs, pointing to their old wounds, telling stories of this or that injury. It was very reassuring for David and everyone else to see this collection of healed scars. The group talked about how kids are able to get hurt and to heal, both in their bodies and in their spirits, their emotions.

Another thing that bothered David and the other kids was the fear of having nightmares. In hushed voices that recalled the terror they had felt, they all complained about their bad dreams. So the group decided to write poems about nightmares, set them to music, and make a scary tape recording of the whole thing. Maybe that would frighten the nightmares away! David explored his fears with this poem:

> One night I woke up out of bed
>   to get a glass of water,
> When a small pink vampire jumped onto me,
>   and next I knew—I fought her.
> She bit me once, I bit her back
>   and fell into a shelf.
> But when I woke up I found out
>   that I had bit myself.

David orchestrated his poem with rhythmic tapping on tonal bamboo pipes, which sounded hauntingly beautiful and lonely.

As the months went by, David's mother's eye continued to

appear in surprising places. The Kids' Arts Group used various sorts of materials to explore death and its impact on their lives. They made a large puppet theater from a refrigerator box, painting it brightly. David added a huge, sad, black-and-blue eye dripping tears all the way to the floor.

The kids also used words to express their thoughts about the loved ones missing from their lives. One day they made "name poems." They wrote the letters of their own names down the left side of a sheet of paper and added words or phrases that described themselves or their fantasies. After that warm-up exercise, they wrote the name of the person who had died, then added descriptive words or phrases.

David's went like this:

H — Having good hope made her last much longer
A — And
R — Really believing made
R — Religious faith stronger.
I — I wish she'd be here, but
E — thEn again I realize, she's happier
T — There, with no cancer, (which I despise)

When David read his name poem, "Harriet," out loud, everyone could hear how far he had come in accepting his mother's death. He added a drawing of her grave, which he had recently visited. It was almost as if he was getting ready to lay her to rest.

Soon after that session, the kids were playing table hockey. David began to draw the eye again while he was waiting for his turn to play. This time when he showed it to the counselor, he was excited and proud of it. The eye was in the center of a large golden spiral, and David had added his mother's initials beneath it. He couldn't say why he had chosen the spiral; he just knew that it felt right.

David asked the counselor to make a photocopy of his spiral. The counselor also looked up spirals in a book about symbols. She found that they appear in the art of every culture known to archaeologists. Spirals always seem to mean the same thing. They signify the concept of infinity, the idea that something eternal lies beyond this physical life we are now living. The way a spiral curves around and around, opening ever outward, represents an aspect of time or the universe that continues forever, without end.

*David's golden spiral containing his mother's eye,
and her initials underneath.*

When the counselor returned the drawing to David, she told him how wonderful it was. And she also told him what she had learned from the book on symbols. He considered this new information for a few quiet minutes. Then he said excitedly, "I know! I put my mother up in heaven, and that's where she belongs." He looked amazed and proud.

And David never drew the eye again.

The last project of the Kids' Arts Group before summer vacation was a quilt. Each child created his or her own special squares. The quilt was meant to show how each person had come to the group with a private pain that death had caused. But when all the individual losses were put together and shared, it made something both beautiful and useful—a healing support group and a wonderful quilt. David's square contained the spiral again, but this

David's quilt square, again containing the spiral but without the eye.

time without the eye. He added "❤ Mom," instead. The whole image was very peaceful—a long, long way from his terrifying cancer faces, glass eyes, flying baseballs, vampires, and graves.

■ CREATIVE SURVIVAL STRATEGIES

Write your name down the side of a sheet of paper, as David did. Can you think of words or phrases that begin with each letter to describe yourself or a fantasy, wish, or hope you have? Write them down, add a few more words to connect the phrases together, then read aloud your name poem. Now try it with the name of a person in your life who has died. Can you remember what you liked about this special person? Can you think of words that describe him or her that start with the name letters? Write them down to create another name poem, then read the words out loud. Does this help you express your feelings for that person you loved? Put both your name poems together and keep them in a special place, like a photo album or journal, where you can add drawings and pictures of the two of you as well.

You can also make a "memory quilt" with your family or a group of friends. Each person chooses a square of material that is his or her favorite color. (Felt squares can be bought already cut at a fabric store.) Then, from other pieces of material, cut a design that expresses how you feel about the person in your life who died. For instance, you might cut out hearts, thunderbolts, or letters that spell out a name. On the square, arrange the pieces into your final design, then carefully turn it over onto a newspaper and lift off the square. This should leave the pieces reversed but in the right places. Next, spray aerosol glue across the newspaper and onto the pieces. Carefully replace the square, patting it onto the sticky pieces. Turn it back over. Pat the pieces down again and let them dry. After all the squares are dry, each one can be placed on a large piece of material, which will be the background. The squares can be sewn directly onto the background material, or sewn together edge to edge and then attached to the backing material, creating a beautiful quilt that can be hung up and treasured.

■ FURTHER EXPLORATIONS

There are a lot of terrible things that can happen to a kid, but one of the worst is to have a mother die. That is what the young hero discovers in *There Are Two Kinds of Terrible*, by Peggy Mann. The twelve-year-old in this book is left living with his father, whom he has seen every day of his life yet hardly knows. He blames his father for not keeping his mother alive somehow, and the two of them fight a great deal. But thanks to shared activities like playing soccer or the drums, they learn to live together in a new way, and to love each other.

Betsy, Amy, & Frankie

Death of a Brother

Betsy leaned over her painting, frowning. She jerked her hand across the canvas board, creating a churning sea of many colors. In the center of her painting was a large white bird flying up toward the left corner. A smaller bird was flying downward in the other direction. "At least the birds are right," she muttered to herself. "They're just like Frankie and me. . . . He's going up, getting out, and I'm going down into this awful ocean."

It didn't seem fair. How could a seventeen-year-old boy be

dying? Well, almost eighteen, she thought. Just four years older than she was. His birthday was next week, and this drawing was his present. Her last present to her brother. Betsy felt proud and sad and angry all at the same time.

The doctors had told her family that what looked like a brain tumor was growing very fast inside Frankie's head. They had given him radiation treatments with powerful X-ray machines to try to shrink the tumor, but it hadn't worked. Soon the tumor would exert such pressure inside his skull that it would shut down his bodily functions, and Frankie would die. Betsy could see what it was already doing to him. Two months ago Frankie had been fine. Then, suddenly, he had had headaches and seizures. After that he couldn't talk very well. Now he hardly spoke at all, and he could barely walk—two people had to hold him up. He was so tall he

Betsy's birthday drawing for her brother Frankie, in which he's flying up and away but she's heading downward.

almost tipped over every time. Frankie needed nurses and aides from the hospice to help his mother and sisters take care of him. And a hospice artist, who was a counselor, came, too—to help the family cope with their feelings about all this change and loss.

The radiation had left Frankie with only a few strands of hair. Though he looked like an old man, Betsy could still see that gleam in his eye sometimes, and Frankie could still make rude gestures when he was mad. Sometimes he joined Betsy and their nine-year-old sister, Amy, at their art sessions, stabbing huge hunks of clay with a fork to vent his anger. As Betsy painted, she could almost hear him make some smart remark like he used to, a remark that would set her giggling in admiration of his daring spirit.

Amy was sitting on the other side of the living room with the hospice artist. She was also painting a birthday present for Frankie. She carefully outlined the letters of his name and filled them in with green paint. Then she made a beautiful rainbow arching over his whole name and painted the background blue. "Dark blue," she said. "Just like I'm feeling. But I hope he likes it, anyway. I hope it makes him smile!"

When they had both finished, Amy said with anticipation, "Let's not wait to give these to him." She went and got Frankie out of his bedroom, pushing him along in the wheelchair he was beginning to use. She handed him the rainbow with his name under it, positively glowing. "Happy birthday, Frankie," she whispered. He stared at it with his haunted eyes and then, as Amy hugged him, he smiled.

Amy's rainbow drawing for Frankie's birthday.

Amy asked the hospice artist to make a drawing of her and Frankie. "So I'll always have *us*." Her sad face looked down on her brother and the thin hand she held so protectively. Frankie seemed to be staring at what lay beyond that room, beyond that moment, perhaps beyond that life.

When the drawing was done, Betsy handed Frankie her painting of the birds. "This is for you, Frankie. You're the big bird flying free! I'm letting you go, Frankie—fly free!" And she gave him a fierce hug while tears poured down her cheeks. Her brother patted her back slowly, nodding his understanding and thanks.

As she lay in his arms, Betsy wondered if her other brother, Billy, would bring Frankie a gift. He had been at reform school for so long, he hardly seemed part of the family. Frankie had spent

a year there, too, for running away and getting in trouble with
the police so many times. Betsy sighed. So much trouble in this
family! She knew her father would never show up, not even for
Frankie's last birthday. He had walked out and left them impov-
erished long ago. After Frankie died, it would just be Betsy and
Amy and their mother. Betsy sighed again, deeply, and cried in
Frankie's stiff, weak arms, wishing this hug could last forever.

The next week they were going to celebrate Frankie's eighteenth birthday. It was likely to be the last celebration before he
died. His family was determined to make it a big bash, with lots
of friends and all the hospice staff who had been taking care of
him. It would be Frankie's way of saying good-bye, too, since he
had always loved a good party. He had gotten caught plenty of
times for having parties without his mother's or other parents'
permission. But this time his mother was in charge.

A few days before his birthday, Frankie became much weaker
—sleeping almost continuously, refusing to get up or to eat. Everyone was worried that he might die before his birthday came.
But Frankie held on. That July day dawned, bright and beautiful,
and Frankie seemed to wake up and glow, too. His mother handed
him a beer and a baseball hat, then wheeled him outside into a
big circle of cheering supporters.

Amy and Betsy were dressed up in costumes, ready to do some
belly dancing with the hospice artist. They had chosen this sort of
dance because they knew Frankie would like the fast, sexy movements, and also because the dance told the story of life, death,

and rebirth through the movements of the arms and torso. They gave Frankie a tambourine to bang on in accompaniment. The Middle Eastern music started, skirts swirled, and multicolored veils enveloped the honored hero of the day. Then the music switched to Frankie's favorite—rock 'n' roll. The girls shook their hips and rang their finger bells. Everyone else laughed and joined in the dancing. Frankie kept the beat from his wheelchair, nodding and smiling, gently tapping the tambourine. People took turns coming over to say hello and give him lots of birthday hugs.

Two weeks later, Frankie died at home. For several days he had been struggling hard for every breath and was restless with the pain in his head. Finally, sufficient morphine gave him some relief from the pain and slowed his breathing down. As his mother held him and as Amy watched from the doorway, he took his last shuddering gasps.

The hospice artist stayed with Amy while her mother went to make the funeral arrangements. Betsy, a day-camp counselor for the summer, had wanted to go to work that morning. She had felt it would be too painful for her to just stand there and watch Frankie die. Amy decided to stay home, but the drawing and painting that she usually enjoyed didn't appeal to her on that hard day. Instead, the hospice artist offered Amy some little cardboard boxes with locking lids. Amy took one and ran upstairs with it. The counselor could hear her rummaging in her favorite drawer full of odds and ends. Five minutes later, she returned with the box and held it out to the artist. Amy had turned it into a tiny bed with a little doll covered by a piece of cloth. It looked like someone in a casket.

"Do you think my mother and the priest will let me put this in Frankie's coffin?" Amy asked. "Because part of me died, too, you know." The hospice artist was struck by Amy's comment and assured her that she would be allowed to do this. The artist told Amy that she was right about a special part of her being gone now that Frankie wasn't here to talk to her, to play with her, to love her. People who love us bring a unique part of ourselves to life, and when they die it can feel as if that special part of us dies, too.

Amy looked thoughtful and asked to go outside for a walk. There she found a few flowers and some special stones, which she added to the box. Amy knew Frankie liked pretty things that came from the earth.

A few months later, when Amy was talking about her burial box to a support group of other kids who had experienced a death in the family, she suddenly said, "But now I really want it *back!*" The group was shocked. "I don't mean that I want to dig it up. But it was a really powerful thing, and I wish I had it back to hold when I think of Frankie."

The hospice artist told Amy that that "powerful thing" could be called a symbol, and that perhaps she could make another one. Amy loved this idea—it made sense to her. Since the group was working with clay, she immediately began modeling several little clay beds, with a clay person covered by a clay blanket on each one. The next week she painted them with the same colors she had used on Frankie's birthday painting. She gave one to the hospice artist and said, "I learned that this symbol can be called a totem, too. In school we studied Native American totems. This totem can give my spirit power and make me feel better when I'm missing Frankie." She cradled the painted clay totem in her hand with a combination of pride and comfort.

However, on other days when the support group met, Amy would draw or paint a sad little girl in a hood, walking all alone. The girl had no hands and no face, just lots of tears pouring out from her. Sometimes Amy would add the words "Why does dying happen?" She was struggling to understand her brother's death. Her drawing symbolized just how helpless she felt, how ashamed

Amy's "Hooded Girl Raining Blood."

Amy's drawing with her question.

to show her face as she walked under a dark cloud, with the sunshine behind her, as though in her past. Amy missed Frankie very much. In a family plagued by loss, the life ahead of her felt bleak without him.

Betsy was sad, too, but also scared and in pain. She recognized that the death of Frankie was just the most recent in a series of tragedies in her family. She still remembered her father beating her brothers and her mother. She knew he had attacked her when she was very young, but she didn't have any memories of it. Her father had divorced her mother when Amy was still a toddler, and they hadn't seen him since. He never sent any money and he didn't even come to Frankie's funeral. What kind of a father was that?

And, of course, her other brother, Billy, had been in trouble for years. What was going to happen to him? Betsy was going to turn fifteen soon, the same age her brothers had been when they ran away and were placed in reform school. Would she have to run away, too? In a few years she'd be eighteen—would she die at that age, too, as Frankie had? No one knew why he had developed a brain tumor. . . . It could happen to her. Her family was such a mess! It seemed like the only good times they had had were when Frankie was dying. What kind of life was that?

All these worries went round and round in Betsy's head. The hospice workers knew enough about them to get her into private counseling. But six months after Frankie died, Betsy tried to kill herself. She stood in the bathroom with pills in one hand, a telephone in the other—and she called her private therapist. He was able to keep her talking on the phone until a mental health worker could get to her house and take her to a hospital.

Betsy knew her therapist and the hospice people cared about her and could help her. She said later she was glad she had made the phone call. She was admitted to a mental health center for two weeks, and the hospice artist visited her there. But two weeks after she went home, she again found herself in the bathroom looking for pills to end her pain. Again she was able to face this terror and save herself by calling for help.

Betsy needed to make sense of what had happened to Frankie, so she wrote the story of Frankie's last months and read it to the kids' support group that she and Amy attended. There everyone knew from personal experience how hard it is when someone you love dies.

It all started in April when my brother Frankie had a seizure. You see Frankie lived in Charlton and the people he was staying with thought he was asleep, but they soon found out he was unconscious. Right when they found out they immediately called an ambulance and he was taken to the hospital, but the doctors couldn't treat him, so they transferred him over to Massachusetts General Hospital.

There at the hospital the team of twelve doctors he had began to run tests. Frankie was still in ICU (Intensive Care) and he was semicomatose. The doctors were still running tests even after he came out of ICU, and into his own room. Then the test results were in and so was the doctors' verdict: Frankie had cancer of the brain and he was going to die.

The doctors also said that because of where the cancer was, it was inoperable, but they were going to try radiation to slow and shrink down the cancer.

I was so glad when Frankie came out of ICU because now I could go and visit him since he had his own room.

By this time Frankie was already into his radiation treatments, and my mother decided that, if he was going to die, he'll die at home. So phone calls were made, and Hospice was brought in to help us. The ball was really rolling, all the equipment and stuff was brought in, and then Frankie came home.

There was never a dull moment with Frankie around, he kept us all on our feet. Because of where the cancer spread Frankie couldn't talk, but he was very alert and you could tell by the look in his eyes he knew what was going on. The doctors told my mother that when she took Frankie home he would not live more than two weeks, were they ever wrong.

Frankie's first nurse was Gloria and boy was she nice. You could tell that Frankie had a crush on her, because when she left and Melissa the aide came in, boy was he ever mad. But after a while he got used to Melissa and I think he liked her a lot.

Since it was June and hot, Frankie could go swimming. The lifeguard would put a life jacket on him and away in the water he'd go, every day he would do this. He would also go for walks outside and kick a soccer ball around.

One time Melissa and a hospice nurse Sandy took Frankie up to the Catskills in upstate New York for the weekend, and when they came back he was so tired he didn't want to get out of bed.

Then July came around and it was soon Frankie's birthday, his eighteenth. It was a fantastic party. Over forty people came, and we even belly danced. I think Frankie liked that best of all. We all knew this was going to be his last birthday but that didn't stop him or us from partying.

> *Then it was August 3. That was the worst day and night. Frankie was in so much pain it just tore me up inside. August 4 wasn't any better either. Then on August 5 before I left for work I looked into his room—he was having such a hard time breathing, I felt so helpless and I kept saying to myself today is going to be the day he dies. And a couple of hours later my boss told me, "Frankie died in your mother's arms at 10 o'clock in the morning."*
>
> *I'll never forget how he fought that cancer. He fought it until he couldn't fight anymore.*

Betsy didn't include what happened to her in the story of Frankie because she understood by then that her suicide attempts were more related to the earlier losses she had experienced at the hands of her father and her brother Billy. Frankie's death had been just one loss too many, but it was one that she could grieve over and lay to rest, while she struggled with her other problems. Frankie's death was the one loss in Betsy's life that was clearly a tragedy and no one's fault. She had participated in his care, celebrated his life, and said good-bye to him in many loving ways. For Betsy, there was closure around Frankie's death. But the pain of having to live with half of her family missing still remained.

Throughout the overwhelming sadness of Frankie's dying, Amy and Betsy knew that celebration and gift-giving were important. Within that tragic situation there was room for laughter and dancing. These were the gifts of life Amy and Betsy gave to Frankie and to themselves. The memory of those good times they will treasure proudly long after his death.

But sometimes the pain of grief can seem unbearable. All you want to do is to get out, to get away from the hurt. At those times the only way out looks like death itself—at least maybe then you can join your loved one. When these feelings come, you need to ask for help. Others who have been through this kind of pain can help you find ways to survive. They can help you understand that you are grieving for something important you have lost, for something you didn't deserve to lose. They know that it can be hard to live without the person you loved or the love you need. But they can give you tools to help resolve these losses and cope with the pain. You can learn to let life in and find meaning, enabling you to love again.

■ CREATIVE SURVIVAL STRATEGIES

Is there someone you need to say good-bye to? Is it hard to find the right words? Try making a present that will show how you feel. Even if that special person is already gone, you can make a good-bye gift that you can treasure for always. Once you have made it, you may find that you want to give it to someone else you love.

Write a story about the someone you loved who died. How did you know this person? What did you like about her or him? Were there times that you didn't get along, things the person said or did that bothered you? Just because people die doesn't mean that they were perfect, or that we have to remember them as perfect. It's important to remember all their human qualities.

How about creating a family celebration? Is there someone who needs a party? Invite your family to lend their ideas. Decorate the party with colored light bulbs. Find some lightweight, flowing material and dance with veils, wrapping them around the special person you want to honor. Do you have any musical instruments for people to play? Ringing bells and banging pots will do nicely! Put on your favorite music and get everybody moving. What else can you add to your Celebration of Life?

■ FURTHER EXPLORATIONS

There is a story for teenagers and adults about a boy whose brother drowns, and who feels so guilty for surviving that he tries to kill himself. *Ordinary People*, by Judith Guest, is a powerful book (made into a movie) about a family's struggle with the dangers of silent grief, and the love that helps a young man decide to live.

Rose

AGE EIGHTEEN

Death of a Father

Rose walked into the school guidance office clutching her sketch-book like a shield. She was shy and pretty, with large trusting eyes. But even when she smiled, as she did now at the hospice counselor, her eyes looked sad. The hospice counselor smiled back and explained that she was an artist who was part of the hospice team taking care of Rose's father.

Rose nodded. She knew. The school guidance counselor had arranged for them to meet at her office. It was more private there than at home. That's what Rose had requested—privacy for help with her artwork and her father's illness.

The counselor asked Rose if she had seen a lot of changes in her father since his struggle with lung cancer had begun a year ago. She nodded again. Quietly, the words came out.

"He used to get up more and work in his shop in the basement. But now he just sits in his chair most of the time. He uses the oxygen machine sometimes." Rose paused. "And I know he's going to die of this," she added, raising her eyes to the counselor's.

"Yes," the counselor agreed, looking straight back. "It's true, he's going to die of this."

Rose seemed to gain courage, and the words came out faster.

"One morning, very early, I heard this screeching sound coming from under my bed. It was the saw running in the basement! My mother and I ran down the stairs and there was my father—he said he just had to get some work done! But he was so shaky he could barely stand. He could have cut his hand off! We got him back to bed and calmed him down, but I'm scared he'll try it again. He's on so much pain medication he doesn't know what he's doing."

How could a teenager cope with this kind of confusion and fear—living with an unpredictable father who was strong enough to get out of bed and do something dangerous, but who was also sick enough to die?

"It must be very scary for you," said the counselor. "Do you know anybody else who has been through this with their father or mother?"

Rose shook her head.

"What helps you feel better when you're worrying about your father?"

"Well . . . I draw some," Rose said, smiling shyly. She slowly unclenched her hands and offered the sketchbook. It was full of her drawings of advertisements, record album covers, and household objects, reflecting her interest in graphic arts. Together, Rose and the counselor went through each page, analyzing it for its strengths and weaknesses. There were also precise, geometric designs she had created to be painted in color on fabrics. Rose explained the origins of her ideas, which came from logos and magazines. With each new page, Rose's smile brightened and her enthusiasm grew.

"These are really good. I can see what you tried to do here, and the colors work well," commented the counselor. "What are you interested in trying next? What about portraits?"

"I've never tried to draw people before," Rose said thoughtfully. When she closed the sketchbook, her face seemed to close up as well. The counselor asked Rose if she would like to get together every week to share her drawings and talk about her father and herself. Rose nodded. Did she need art supplies, the counselor wanted to know. The hospice could buy them for her. Rose smiled and said her family never had much money and now things were worse. So they made a list of materials to get, such as thick paper, colored pencils, and charcoal.

When Rose walked out the door into the crowded, noisy hallway, she was once again armed with her sketchbook shield and a small, sad smile.

As the weeks passed, and Rose grew more comfortable in the counselor's company, she began to talk about her relationship with her father. The counselor already knew, from the school guidance counselor, that Rose had brought a charge of abuse against her father last year. She had told the school, the police, and the state department of social services that he was touching her inappropriately. This accusation had turned Rose's family upside down. But six months later, when her father became sick with cancer, Rose dropped the charge. Why did Rose change her mind about prosecuting him? It was important to find out in order to help Rose understand what her father's dying meant to her.

"I am the youngest of five kids, but everyone has moved out of the house now except me. My dad used to fight with everybody. He even hit my mother. But not me. I was his favorite. He used to teach me how to do woodwork and let me help him make the dog houses and glider swings we sold from our front yard.

"But two years ago, he started touching me where he shouldn't. Whenever I'd walk by, he'd reach out and grab me. I told him to cut it out—that he'd better stop! But he didn't. And one night, when my mother was out, he tried to get into my room. I blocked the door with my dresser so he couldn't get in, but he broke the doorjamb! I couldn't lock my door anymore. I was so scared that he would get in. . . . Every night I would move my dresser in front of the door to protect myself from him.

"I told my mother and my family about all this. My mother was scared, but my brothers and sister, who all live nearby, didn't believe me. They thought I was making up lies, and they were angry. And then one day, my youngest brother saw Dad grab me in the kitchen. So he told everyone it was true. The authorities made me move out of the house. My mom came with me, and we went to my sister's house. Then everyone was really mad at me for making so much trouble!

"But then my dad got sick, and when we went to visit him he stopped bothering me. So we dropped the subject and moved back to take care of him. And now he's dying!"

Rose was full of anger, frustration, relief, and guilt. She still loved her father. But her sadness about his dying was mixed with her feelings about his abusing her sexually. Part of her hated him, another part loved him, and part of her felt guilty for the trouble and upset her family claimed she had caused. Rose wondered if her actions had brought on her father's cancer.

The counselor asked Rose to think about how she could say good-bye to her father before he died. "What do you need to say to him now so you won't regret losing this opportunity after he is gone?"

"I know I have to settle things somehow," Rose admitted. "I

don't want to be bothered the rest of my life by these memories and awful feelings."

Together, they tried practicing what Rose might like to say to her father. She tried to imagine who would need to be with her to make her feel safe. Her boyfriend? Her mother? The counselor? But as she thought about it, Rose realized the idea of an actual confrontation with her father didn't feel right. She didn't want to show her father her angry feelings when he was lying in bed, dying. During the years of his violent outbursts, Rose had always hidden in her room to avoid the scenes. She had never been able to show him her anger, and she didn't want to start now.

The counselor suggested Rose keep a journal in which she could write about her father and draw pictures of him. She could explore her feelings for him in words and art, instead of confronting him. Rose found this easier to do. She drew his face in profile, with half of him hidden, just as he seemed to her in life. The good part showed, while the scary, secret, grabbing part of him was hidden—from everyone except her. She drew his eyes closed and his mouth open, making him look vulnerable and in pain. Her writing described his strange behavior during his illness and the disappointment she felt with him for not being a "true father." But Rose stopped short of writing about her anger. Perhaps as she wrote, her recollections of her father and his behavior still left her feeling unsafe.

Rose continued to draw and write in her journal often. She showed the entries to the counselor during their weekly sessions.

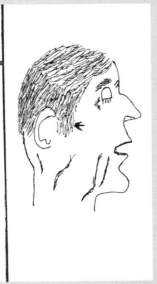

Dad sitting on the living chair. He was sleeping on the chair. He was talking in he's sleep; grabing for stuff that was not really there. Sometimes he would wake up scared and not knowing were he was. Sometimes he acted like he was hammering. I feel sorry for him. I know he is not in any pain but it bugs me seeing him this way! I wish he would go away fast so I wouldn't see him this way. He was always a hard worker. He would still work if he was in pain. He never took pills until now. You would always see him working. It bugs me seeing him seating there all day doing nothing. He wouldn't do anything with us like other fathers would with their kids so he wasn't a true father to me. All he would do is complain about everything you would do.

Rose's drawing of her father, with her thoughts.

Her subjects included her youngest brother, who had been a good support for her during the last two years. He had believed her after he had witnessed the abuse, and he had stood up for her to the rest of the family. She also drew horrible monster faces, saying, "That's how I feel when I get up in the morning." She put a lot of her anger and disgust into those gargoyle faces. Another picture showed an open road curving up the page, with rocks and bushes along the way.

"If you were walking along this road you've drawn," the counselor asked, "where would you be right now?"

Rose pointed to a spot behind a boulder.

"Between a rock and a hard place?" the counselor asked.

Rose nodded sadly. It was the right image for Rose's dilemma.

This is me when I don't want to get up in the maring!

Rose's monster face expresses some of the feelings inside her.

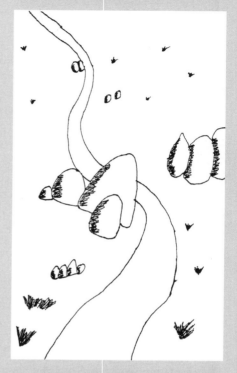

Rose's "Rocky Road" shows there are barriers to the choices she can make.

To help Rose sort out how to say good-bye to a father who had hurt her, the counselor encouraged Rose to try to recall and talk about her father's behavior in more detail. Where did he touch you on your body? What room were you in when it happened? How often did it happen? For how long did this go on? What was his facial expression? How soon did you tell? Who was responsible for this molestation? What did you lose during this whole experience? If Rose could let herself remember the specific incidents and her feelings at the time, maybe that would give her the strength and clarity to hold her father accountable. Then she could say a clean, clear good-bye.

As Rose talked, it became clear that after the first few times her father had surprised her by grabbing her breasts and buttocks, she had been able to stop him when he tried to molest her again—first by pushing him away and saying no, then by hiding, finally by telling others. She had prevented him from removing her clothes and violating her further. What *was* fully violated was her trust—in her father and in the family members who refused to believe her or thought she was making a big deal out of nothing.

The counselor helped Rose see what a good job she had done defending herself. Any blame or shame belonged to her father for doing something he had no right to do, and to her brothers and sister for punishing her for their father's actions and the repercussions.

Often the counselor tried to get Rose to express the anger she might feel about all of this by using words or drawings or clay. But each time Rose denied feeling any rage at her father's betrayal. Rose could put some of her anger into her gargoyle faces, but the rest was turned into resignation and depression. She did not feel safe enough or justified enough to express her anger at her father in words or gestures or fantasies. Perhaps she was afraid of losing the love she still had for him, the very thing she wanted most to keep after he was gone.

So Rose was left only with sensations of frustration, sadness, and emptiness. To survive in a violent household, she had spent her life covering up her feelings. During this difficult time, she could not change. As her father's cancer grew worse, it was too much to ask that she handle her sorrow, guilt, and anger all at once.

Five months went by and Rose's father slowly drew closer to death. He became totally dependent on an oxygen machine and could move around only as far as its plastic line permitted. When he was asleep, his eyelids didn't close completely, and Rose could see the whites of his eyeballs as they rolled up into his head. His chest sounded hollow; each breath rattled in his throat, leaving small bubbles at the corners of his mouth. Rose stared at him and knew it was time to resolve the question of good-byes. She played out each possible scene of confrontation or forgiveness privately, in her mind, and then spoke to the counselor.

"He's suffered enough," she said. "I can forgive him now, without wanting to hurt him back. I've gotten the feelings out of me as much as I can, so I just want to be sad about his dying, and not be angry about the way he lived."

Rose was proud of herself for being able to give her father this last gift—her forgiveness, and with it a more peaceful death. Rose's father died quietly at home, surrounded by his family and the hospice caregivers.

After he died, no one included Rose in the funeral plans. Whether the family was trying to protect her or to punish her,

Rose felt hurt and left out. But she decided to participate anyway. During the wake at the funeral home, she put some of her favorite things in her father's coffin—a rose, for which her father had named her at birth; a photograph of them together; and a drawing of a rose she had made for him. Then she wrote a speech to read at his funeral the next day. She told her mother and the priest that she was going to read it. In these ways, Rose said her good-byes. She was pleased that she could talk about her father in front of so many people. She felt free to express sadness and compassion for a difficult man, without feeling any guilt.

Life after her father's death was very hard, with little money and many worries for Rose's family. The hospice counselor and Rose worked on these new problems of survival by exploring how

Rose's last drawing for her father.

she could earn money now and in the future. Rose's school guidance counselor signed her up for a summer youth employment program, and the hospice counselor took her to the interview. Rose was shy but clear about her abilities and willingness to work, and she got a job. She would be paid to teach crafts to people with Alzheimer's disease at an adult day care center. It was a good job for Rose's talents. In addition, the counselor helped her shop for beading kits and other new materials so Rose could teach herself to make earrings and necklaces to sell to kids at school in the fall. Rose's guidance counselor also enrolled her in a specialized program that would give her extra training in graphic arts during her senior year. They hoped this would prepare her for a job in the printing industry after graduation.

Rose taught herself how to paint on fabrics and do beadwork with the kits she bought. Fashioning her intricate, beautiful jewelry designs took a lot of time and concentration, and Rose said this relieved her mind. She would remember her father lying in bed, using oxygen and struggling to breathe. The times he tried to molest her seemed now to Rose to be part of his illness. She felt he must have been sick in his mind to do something like that. And then he got sick in his body. The two events were connected for Rose by the guilt she thought he should feel and the punishment she thought he did receive by having cancer.

Rose worried about her mother's health and helped around the house as much as possible. She missed the closeness she and her father had shared, working together on projects in the basement;

she wished those times could have continued. But doing her own projects now connected her to those past times and gave her similar feelings of satisfaction.

Rose decided to make a wooden treasure box in which to keep special objects that reminded her of her father. She worked hard sanding and shellacking and resanding, until finally the wood felt as smooth as velvet. She knew her father would have approved of her work. She showed the box to the hospice counselor with the photos and mementos she had put in it. Rose said she knew her memory and love for her father would never get lost now, no matter how many changes came into her life.

It is very hard to grieve for someone we have both loved *and* hated. This ambivalence—this feeling of going back and forth between opposite emotions—cannot be ignored. Before Rose could say good-bye to her father, she had to find ways to deal with the deep hurt he had caused her. Talking about what happened with a safe outsider, writing and drawing in a journal—these activities gave her the safety, freedom, and distance to explore her emotions without fear of consequences or punishment.

But even that permission is not always enough to express feelings that are powerful and deeply hidden. Rose experienced how hard it is to feel anger at a dying parent, however justified that anger is. She was able to recognize the loss of trust, the unfairness of the hurts, and the responsibility for the damage that belonged to others, not to her. Thus she was relieved of any guilt she might feel for hating her father. This helped her to forgive him.

But it may take years before she is fully aware of just how angry she was, before she believes that she is entitled to her anger. Or she may never be able to let those feelings into her life. Maybe one day, Rose will look into her treasure box and be able to admit her anger without losing her love. Then it will be possible to say a truly complete good-bye to her father, and grieve the loss of what might have been.

■ CREATIVE SURVIVAL STRATEGIES

Is there a parent or sibling or someone else in your life who is hard to talk to? Do you want to be closer to this person but don't quite know how? Try creating a "shared journal" with that person. Choose a blank book, one that attracts your eye and feels good in your hands. Find a ribbon to use as a bookmark. Keep the book in your room until you are ready to write. Then put down a thought or draw an image or both—whatever occurs to you— and mark the page with the ribbon. Leave the book in a place you and the other person have agreed on. That person will read the journal when she or he is ready. The second person will write in it eventually, mark the entry with the ribbon, and return it to the special place. In this way you both can communicate without talking face-to-face, which can sometimes be so hard to do. What do you need to tell this person? Can you write about the good feelings you have for him or her? Has anything made you angry? Has anyone ever hurt you or touched you in a way that felt wrong to you? Can you write these things down in this shared journal? What responses do you get? Keep the secret journal journeying back and forth.

If you have been touched inappropriately, it's very important to tell a trusted adult. And if you don't get a supportive response from that person, tell another adult. You deserve help in maintaining your safety. You have a right to this, and a right to pursue it until you get this help.

You can also make your own treasure box. Find an empty box like one for cigars, or an unused toolbox, an old jewelry box, or a shoe box—any container that feels right to you. Glue soft fabric inside the box, or paint the outside, or make a collage of pictures and words to decorate it—anything so long as it becomes your own special box. Collect things that represent people or pets you loved who have died. Put these objects inside—objects like special photos, rocks, shells, gifts, a collar, anything that will fit. This is your treasure box. It can receive all the precious mementos that will remind you of the people or pets you miss throughout your life.

■ FURTHER EXPLORATIONS

Rose felt alone and isolated after her father's death. She didn't know any other people who had gone through what she was experiencing. So she read *How It Feels When a Parent Dies*, by Jill Krementz. In each chapter, accompanied by photographs, a different child or teenager tells of the death of a parent. When you read these young people's powerful stories and share their feelings, you'll know you're not alone in your pain.

Jesse, Renee, & Gabe

AGES THIRTEEN, NINE, AND FOURTEEN

Accidental Death of a Mother

It was getting late. Thirteen-year-old Jesse looked out the window again, but it was too dark to see much except the light from the porch and the shadowy outlines of the other houses on the quiet little street where she lived. Ten o'clock. Her mother wasn't home yet, and Jesse was worried. This afternoon her mom had left to visit her boyfriend, who was in prison. She had said she'd be back by eight o'clock. Of course, her mother had been late before. But something felt different about tonight.

Jesse remembered this afternoon. She and her mother had argued about the visit. They had both gotten furious. When her mother left, slamming the door behind her, Jesse had felt a shiver go down her spine. I'll never see her again! she had thought.

But that's silly, she told herself now. Maybe I just didn't want to see her again because I was mad at her. Jesse knew a social worker had warned her mother that if she took up with her boyfriend again—a convicted child beater—Jesse and her brother and sister would have to go back into foster care. "And we just got back home a month ago! Why would she risk losing us again?" Jesse wondered aloud. Anger flooded through her, shoving her frightening premonition deep down inside.

Jesse had put her nine-year-old sister to bed over an hour ago. But Renee had awakened with a bad dream, so she was now on the couch, curled up asleep next to their fourteen-year-old brother, Gabe. He was engrossed in a science fiction novel.

Suddenly the phone rang, shaking the silence. Gabe answered. Jesse could tell by her brother's voice that it was *him*. No, their mother wasn't back yet. What time had she left the prison? Six o'clock? That was hours ago! She should have been home by now. Jesse swallowed hard, trying to keep the fear out of her throat. Gabe hung up, and she and her brother looked at each other in silent dread.

A knock on the door made them both jump. When Jesse and her brother opened the door they were almost not surprised to see a police officer standing there. He asked if an adult was at home. When they answered that they were home alone, he told them to call an adult. Gabe shakily dialed the number of the foster parents he had last stayed with. They said they would come right over. They also said they would bring the social worker who had helped the children twice before, when their mother had been hospitalized for nervous breakdowns.

While they all waited, the officer wouldn't answer any questions. He stood staring silently at the sleeping Renee. Finally the foster parents and the social worker arrived. The officer took them into a separate room and shut the door. Renee woke up and asked what was happening, but Jesse and Gabe had no answers. Then the adults returned. The social worker said that she was very sorry to have to tell the children that their mother had been killed in an automobile accident at seven o'clock that evening. Her car had swerved into an oncoming gravel truck. The driver had not been able to avoid hitting her. The social worker went on to say that she would stay overnight with them, and then tomorrow Jesse, Renee, and Gabe would all pack their things and move into Gabe's foster parents' home, in a nearby town.

Jesse thought, This can't be true. . . . I'm dreaming! But it was a nightmare she couldn't wake from. There were no close relatives to take care of them. Their father had been separated from the family years ago for beating his children, and they hadn't heard from him since. Suddenly Jesse, Gabe, and Renee were like orphans. In one night, they had lost not only their mother but their home, their school, and their friends. Their lives would be changed in almost every way, and this time their mother was gone forever.

Two months later Jesse, Gabe, and Renee were all still living with Gabe's foster parents in a nice ranch house with plenty of room. The foster parents were a young childless couple who were considering keeping the children permanently. But they were worried about what they called Renee's "obsession" with drawing pictures of deaths and illnesses of all kinds, and with the older children's silence about their mother. The social worker asked a hospice counselor to visit Jesse, Gabe, and Renee "to help them with their grief."

The counselor met all three children together and settled down on the floor of Renee and Jesse's room for privacy. She passed out paper and large colored markers that smelled like different fruits. The kids took turns sniffing the markers and guessing the flavors.

"It's easier to talk when your hands are busy drawing," the counselor said. "I know your mother died. And I know death changes a family because my brother died, too, and everything changed after that. Can you tell me what happened?" Slowly, the children told the story of the long waiting and wondering on the terrible night of their mother's accident. They spoke softly but in a matter-of-fact manner. There were no tears, no anger, not even sad faces—just stunned, cautious looks. But their drawings showed what was going on inside of them.

Nine-year-old Renee gleefully drew cats being squashed by trucks, toilets on fire, and people's eyeballs falling out. She called the drawing "Bulimia, Pneumonia, and Whiplash," and said her foster parents wouldn't tell her how to spell those words. The counselor spelled them out for her and asked about the drawings. Yes, her mother's car had been squashed by a truck. And Renee knew the word "bulimia" because Jesse had been reading a book for health class about a girl who had bulimia and threw up in toilets. Now that her mother had died in a car crash, Renee was curious about other ways to die. By drawing these disasters, she could release and even control the words and images that might

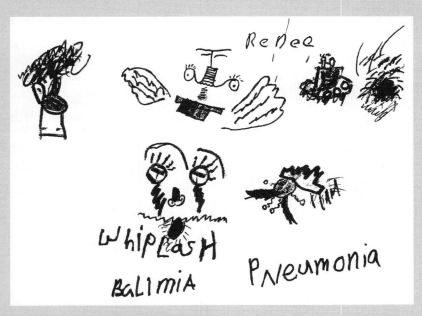

Renee's "Bulimia, Pneumonia, and Whiplash" shows the disaster and destruction that are on her mind.

be frightening her. This control gave her some comfort, after the total loss of control that her mother's death had created in their lives.

Gabe had a fantasy novel with him, which he talked to the counselor about. He had read all of Tolkien's trilogy and Herbert's Dune series, and he was now trying out other writers. The stories he liked were full of fantastic places and powerful magic. As he talked about these books and how they helped him to escape his troubled life, Gabe drew a magic "flaming sword" that could protect him. He added a "pearl of wisdom" to the handle, explaining that this would help him recognize both his enemies and his allies.

Jesse was more reserved than her brother and sister. She silently drew a homeless man without shoes walking toward a garbage

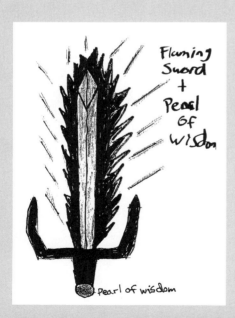

Gabe's drawing of the sword that will keep him safe.

can. In the background, behind a barricading fence, was a broken-down house with a shattered window. When the counselor asked her if she felt like this man, she nodded vigorously. "See? He's got no home, no shoes, and now he's going to have to fight the cat for the garbage to eat!"

The counselor asked how Jesse was feeling about her mother's death. Jesse shrugged. "How can you think about a dead mother when you don't know where your next clean socks are coming from?" Although for the moment Jesse was well fed and well groomed, her anxiety over whether that might suddenly change in the next week or the next month was intensely real. Jesse told the counselor that she and her brother and sister had been in foster care before. Their mom had even considered giving them up again,

Jesse's deep feelings of abandonment and fears about the future are revealed in her drawing of a homeless man.

just before she died. The children knew it was possible that their mother had intentionally driven into the truck—that she had committed suicide. But now, while they were so vulnerable, it was impossible to face this abandonment directly. It didn't feel safe to let go and cry a lot or get really mad. Instead of being angry, the children feared more abandonment and loss.

There were so many changes in their lives that Jesse, Renee, and Gabe could barely think about how much they missed their mother, or how to say good-bye to her now that she was dead. There was a new school to go to—at a time when it was hard to concentrate and hard to make new friends. They had been back to visit their old neighborhood once, but that was painful and awkward, too. No one knew what to say to them, and they didn't feel like they belonged there anymore.

Jesse said it was only when she was alone at night, lying in bed, that she could let herself think about her mother and their old apartment. Then she would realize that she would never go back there, that her mother would never come back. Sadness and anger would flood through her. But she felt she had to be careful during the daytime and not show her feelings. Otherwise, she and her brother and sister might get kicked out of this new home. None of them felt safe enough to take a chance sharing emotions.

The counselor hugged each of the children and reassured them that they didn't deserve all this tragedy and pain. "You are great kids and I wish I could bring your mother back," the counselor said. "But that's not within my power. The most I can do is provide a feeling of safety when we're were together once a week, and help you learn ways to carry your own sense of safety inside of you."

The next time she came, the kids met the counselor at the door. She gave them each a hardcover journal with blank pages inside. "When you write and draw in this book, it will help you untangle your feelings. Putting yourself into words and pictures will make you feel stronger and less confused. Your journal will be there whenever you need someone to talk to, no matter where you go."

Jesse, Renee, and Gabe took the books gladly. They decorated the covers with individual designs cut from metallic papers. Then they started to draw and write their thoughts and feelings. Renee drew what she called "a treasure chest for all my precious jewels." But after she noticed that the chest looked like a coffin, she decided to leave the jewels outside of it, where they would be safer. Instead of treasure, she filled the box with jagged red marks and called it "a loving chest." But the agitated lines looked more like blood and pain than love.

Jesse discovered through her journal that she could write poetry. Words and ideas seemed to flow out of her and act like Gabe's sword, protecting her and keeping her hopes alive. She wrote about her need to strengthen herself for the future: "Me, Myself and I, You'll never be lonely if you have Me, Myself and I." She drew idyllic mountains and meadows, always with a large tree stump in the foreground, cut off from its life as Jesse

Renee's "loving chest."

felt she had been. Then she would add the words of her poems below the scene.

Here I sit
All alone.
Here I sit
I have no home.
Here I sit.
Here I wonder,
Here I ponder
What colorful thoughts.
Here am I.
Here, Why?

Jesse wrote whatever occurred to her, without any assignment or suggestions. Within these pages she was free and secure. On a more hopeful day she created the idea of a "Love Fixer."

Sometimes wishes and dreams don't always come true.
And yet we wonder why?
Still, no explanation.
All we can do is keep wishing and hoping and dreaming.

Sometimes we lose someone we love.
The weird emptiness that fills us.
You can never replace a lost love, but you can mend it.
Can you imagine a Love Fixer?

This world needs more Lovers and Dreamers.

As the months went on, Gabe got busy with Boy Scouts and sought a safe escape in his reading. Renee found it easy to make new friends and become close to her foster parents. But Jesse was shy, withdrawn, and angry. She often fought with her brother and was more isolated than her sister. Her silent suffering showed that she needed the journal writing and extra support even more than her siblings.

One day the counselor, who was pregnant, came for a visit close to the date when her baby was due. Renee looked at the counselor's big belly and asked if she could feel the baby move. The counselor lay down on the floor, took Renee's hand, and helped her feel the baby turning over to adjust to the mother's new position. Jesse watched, silent but intent. The counselor asked her if she would also like to feel the baby move. "No, no thanks," she said. "I'm sure I will have one soon enough!"

Her answer surprised the counselor—Jesse was only thirteen. Was she really thinking about having a baby? But then it made sense. It must be tempting to create someone to love you, someone to whom you can give all your love, when you are so very alone in the world, as Jesse felt herself to be. But for children to make children is a dangerous solution to loneliness. It is hard on both the babies and the mothers to be young and unsupported in this world.

The counselor asked Jesse if she thought it would help her to have a baby to love. But Jesse wouldn't talk about it. She did accept a hug from the counselor and relaxed in her arms for a while.

The counselor continued to visit Jesse, Renee, and Gabe for four months. The last time she saw them they had just been told their foster care arrangement had fallen apart. The foster parents were getting a divorce. The social worker involved thought the children would do better apart. Besides, she knew it would be easier to find homes for them if they were separated. Foster parents who would be willing to take on one child might not take on three.

The social services department also discontinued the visits from the counselor. "The children should be ready to move on into their new lives," the authorities said, despite the objections of the counselor. The only thing she could do was write her phone number on the inside of each child's journal. All of this meant more losses for Jesse, Renee, and Gabe—different families, different routines, different schools. And now they wouldn't even have one another. They didn't know where they would be placed—they could be hours and miles apart. It was hard to imagine how the three of them would adjust.

That last day Jesse drew a little person standing next to a suitcase, looking back, surrounded by three poems.

> *"Rebel"*
> *When I die*
> *I'm sure*
> *I will have a*
> *Big Funeral . . .*
> *Curiosity Seekers*
> *Coming to see*
> *If I*
> *Am really*
> *Dead . . .*
> *Or just*
> *Trying to make*
> *Trouble.*

Jesse was angry. She wondered whether anyone would care if she died. She wondered whether she was a troublemaker. Perhaps everything was being taken away from her as a punishment. Or perhaps she was also referring to her mother's funeral—was her mother really dead or "just trying to make trouble"? In any case, her mother's death *had* made trouble.

> *"Question"*
> *Why isn't there*
> *A light bulb*
> *On top of*
> *Your Head*
> *That lights*
> *Up every*
> *Time . . .*

The counselor tried to get Jesse to answer the questions "*When would the light bulb light up? Why would you need a signal?*" But Jesse couldn't say. Then, as they hugged each other for the last time, they both knew the light bulb question was about this —the warmth and affection Jesse needed so much. How would strangers know when this quiet, awkward adolescent needed a hug? How would she get the love she needed, the counselor wondered. Too bad there wasn't a light bulb that would just light up!

  The last poem, "A Choice of Weapons," stands as a powerful testament to the needs of children in pain.

Sticks and stones are hard on bones,
Aimed with angry art.
Words can sting like anything,
But silence breaks the heart.

This altered childhood rhyme recalls the blows that Jesse had to take in life—and the words that hurt her, too. But it is the silence—of a dead mother, of others around Jesse who are unable to hear her and respond, and of her own inability to ask for help—all this silence that breaks her heart.

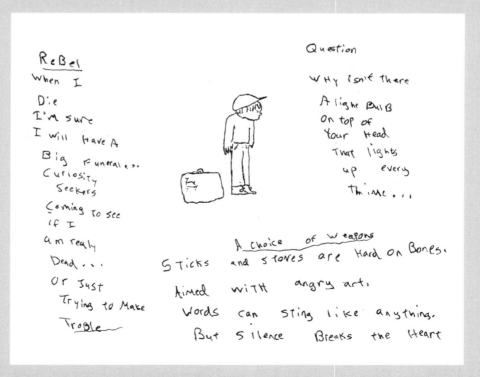

Jesse's last poems before the kids had to split up.

Even in the face of extreme loss of so many kinds, there was room in Jesse for hope. She had found a voice for her suffering and fears in her writing. Because she could write her poems and then choose someone special with whom to share them, she had a means of finding more help, hope, and love in her unknown future.

■ CREATIVE SURVIVAL STRATEGIES

If you keep a journal, write a "Fears and Hopes" poem. It can be about what you are afraid might happen to you, and how you can stay hopeful when you are scared. When change and loss come into our lives and take some of our dreams away, it is important to create *new* hopes and wishes. Then we have a chance to make them come true. The future can still be something to look forward to. What new wishes and dreams for your future can you put in your journal?

You can also create your own "magic shield." Go to your favorite pizza place and ask for one of their big, round, cardboard pizza plates (before it has been used). Decorate your shield by choosing symbols that make you feel powerful, safe, and protected. Draw and paint them onto the shield, or glue on feathers, sequins, magazine photographs and words, cloth scraps—anything you can think of to make your shield a truly powerful, protective image of yourself! When you are done, tape a six-inch-by-one-inch strip of arched cardboard to the center of the back as a handle.

■ FURTHER EXPLORATIONS

When their mother died, it was so sudden that Jesse, Renee, and Gabe never got a chance to say good-bye. Is that worse than watching someone you love die slowly, day by day? This is one of the themes in Judy Blume's *Tiger Eyes*, a book about two friends who have both lost their fathers. One father was shot in a robbery; the other boy's dad died painfully of a cancer that slowly changed everything about him. Both characters explore the issue of how to say good-bye after the person is already dead, and which kind of death is the hardest to endure.

Jessica, Jason, & David

AGES TEN, NINE, AND SIX

Death of a Father

Three children sat drawing at the kitchen table, while a visiting hospice counselor kept them supplied with paper and markers. Suddenly, nine-year-old Jason jumped up from the table, crumpled a piece of paper, and threw it on the floor, where it joined three other balls of frustration. "I can't do it! I just can't draw today!"

The counselor tried to soothe him. "You don't have to," she said. "Do you want to go outside and run around for a while?" But Jason shook his head violently and sat back down. He stared at his brother and sister, kicking his chair in rhythmic anger.

Ten-year-old Jessica also looked sulky. She was silently working on a drawing, which she hid in the crook of her arm. Only six-year-old David seemed happy to be coloring a picture of his father. He knew his daddy was very sick and was soon going to die and live in heaven—his mom had told the whole family that. But David wasn't sure what this meant. For the moment he was just glad to have his daddy home from the hospital. Now he could see him whenever he wanted.

Meanwhile, Jason couldn't sit still; he couldn't bring himself to leave the kitchen and he couldn't stay there, either. He was so full of energy and emotion that he didn't know what to do. The counselor tried again, this time inviting him to create a "duo drawing" with her. First, she made a shape on the paper—a crescent moon with a jagged edge, like Jason's energy. Then she asked Jason to add something to the drawing.

Jason stared a minute, then pounced on the paper. Turning it around, he drew a handle that changed the moon into a pickax. Next, the counselor added a long horn shape down the side of the paper. Jason drew jagged lines coming out of it, like the angry, blaring sound he would have made if he were that horn. By then Jason knew what the picture should be, and he took over. Behind the pickax he added a big face with a black mark over the mouth. When the counselor asked about the mouth, Jason explained, "That's my dad. He's been yelling at me all day!" Then he drew four faces at the bottom of the page, all connected to a dark whirling pool that threatened to drown them. Only one face was smiling. "That's David," said Jason. "Look at him—the whole family is miserable and he's happy! He doesn't even know what's going on!"

Jason loved his father dearly, but he was struggling with his anger at him. A brain tumor was killing his dad, changing his personality, taking him further and further away from Jason and the other children every day. His father's face was so swollen from the medicine and radiation treatments that he didn't even look like himself. He didn't get out of bed much anymore. He just lay there and yelled at everyone.

Jason's "duo drawing" expresses his anger over his father's illness and the changes it is causing.

Six-year-old David ignored his older brother, finished his drawing, and proudly showed it to the counselor. "See, it's called 'Daddy and Jesus Talking Up in Heaven.' Daddy is the one with the frown because he's not sure he wants to be in heaven, and Jesus is doing all the talking!"

The counselor asked why Daddy and Jesus had no legs and were sitting on the edge of their chairs. David said, "Up in heaven you don't need legs—everybody flies. But then when they sit down they might fall off the chairs. Jesus knows about this and he's hanging on. But Daddy doesn't know. Do you think he'll fall out of heaven?" David looked worried now, and he went to talk to his mother and find out more about this heaven where his daddy was going—like how you got up there and if you could fall out.

David's drawing of his father up in heaven talking to Jesus.

On other days Jessica had also drawn images of her father up in heaven. In one, he had his back to her. He was playing the piano, surrounded by angels who were singing and accompanying him on instruments. Jessica had loved to play the piano with her father. She knew the two of them wouldn't be playing together up in heaven after he died.

On this day, Jessica finished her drawing, then turned it face-down and scribbled on the back angrily. But she let the counselor gently turn the paper over to see what Jessica had drawn that upset her so. Jessica's father was dressed for work, complete with shirt and tie. But he had no feet—how could he get to work? In reality, her father hadn't been to work in months. As in David's drawing, the missing limbs showed that something was wrong with their dad, that he was no longer the person he used to be. Jessica had drawn him with ears but then had erased them. Like Jason, she was upset with her dad's yelling. She felt he wasn't listening to her.

Jessica couldn't bear to destroy her father's face on the front of the paper, so she had scribbled out her anger on the back. She had always been his special girl. She was used to hearing her dad yell at Jason, but he had never yelled at *her* like that until today. Jessica knew her father couldn't help being sick. She knew he didn't want to die. But she was hurt and saddened by the sudden change in him all the same.

Three different siblings, three different drawings, three different sets of feelings—all existing at the same moment, in the same

*Jessica's drawing of her dad, with some of her
angry scribbling on the back showing through.*

home, about the same dying father. It was a painful reality that
brought Jessica, Jason, and David closer to one another and to
their mother. Yet their separate worries, pains, and normal com-
petition also pulled them apart.

About a week later, their mom told the three children that their
father was unconscious and having trouble breathing. He would
probably die that day. They all went to his bed, and each said
good-bye with hugs and kisses and tears. Together they decided
to do one of their dad's favorite things—take a ride and get ice-
cream cones. They just couldn't stay there and watch him die.
They didn't want to see it, and their mother thought it would be
better to go out and honor their father's life by doing something

he had always enjoyed. They knew he wouldn't be alone; the hospice nurse was there to stay with him until the end.

When the family came back a few hours later, the nurse told them that their dad had died. David rushed to the bed, climbed on top of his father's big, silent body, and sobbed his heart out. Jessica and Jason joined their mom at the bedside. They hugged her while she rubbed David's back until he had cried himself out. Then her warm arms held her youngest son as they all said their last good-byes to their father.

Jason was often angry about many things after his father died. Filled with rage, standing up and shouting at everyone, he could turn his classroom upside down in a minute. And he could ruin a family dinner even faster by yelling at his brother and sister or telling his mother that his dad would have done things differently. His mother called him "the family barometer." Jason's behavior measured what the other family members were also feeling but could not directly reveal.

Jason and David joined a children's support group called Kids' Arts led by the hospice counselor who had visited them when their father was dying. There they met other children who were trying to cope with the death of a parent. During the meetings, Jason often drew pictures that showed rage darkening his eyes, giving him a furious power as he pounded a punching bag: "POW!" Sometimes his drawings were of men in armor, totally protected from the outside world and dangerous to others.

"Jason, do you ever feel you'd like to live inside the armor that you draw?" the counselor asked him one day.

"Yeah. Then nothing and nobody could hurt me anymore!" declared Jason.

"I can understand why you might want this extra protection now. But what would happen if you lived inside that armor and you got hungry?"

"Well . . . I guess I'd have to drink my food or only eat mushy stuff because there's no room to chew." Jason frowned. The armor idea might need some adjusting.

"And what if you wanted to hug someone?" continued the counselor. "Or what if someone wanted to hug *you?* What would happen?"

Jason's angry feelings come out in his "Pow!" drawing.

"I think all my sharp armor might hurt that person," he said with a look of consternation.

"Maybe that's what is happening to you now, in your family and at school. Maybe you're trying so hard to protect yourself that you aren't getting the love that you need. And the love that people want to give you." The counselor asked the group, "How can we protect ourselves in ways that don't hurt us?"

After much discussion, Jason and the group designed a "magic vest" that was made of velvet and silk and decorated with symbols they all liked. Stars were for the new wishes they needed to make so that their dreams could come true in the future. A rainbow symbolized the promise that life would get better for them. A dove stood for peace. It also stood for the freedom to escape from

Jason's need to feel strong and protected shows in his armor drawing.

difficult feelings by expressing them creatively. After the kids made the magic vest, it sat on an empty chair during every meeting. Anytime anyone felt the need for more protection, he or she could go put it on. This also let the counselor and the other kids know that the person needed some hugs and reassurance.

Sometimes Jason and David would fight and argue in the support group. Then the counselor would see that it was time to play Guided Combat. This was a hitting game played with foam bats. The kids would all pair up and listen to the rules: you have to say what you're mad at before you hit your partner with the foam bat; no hitting above the shoulders; the fighting stops when anyone yells, "Time out!" David and Jason would start off while the rest of the group cheered them on, calling out, "What are you mad about?"

"I'm mad at you, David!" shouted Jason.

"Well, I'm mad at you, too—you always yell at me!"

"Come on, what are you *really* mad about?" the counselor asked from the sidelines.

"I'm mad at my teacher and the principal!" shouted Jason as he hit David with the foam bat.

"Why are you mad at them? What did they do?"

"They *told everyone* that my dad was dead!" yelled Jason.

"And I'm mad that my dad *is dead!*" added David, smacking Jason at the knees.

"Yeah! I'm mad at God for letting my dad die!" answered

Jason. After a few more blows, the two brothers fell into a bean-bag chair, exhausted and, for now, rid of their bad feelings.

Expressing this last anger—being mad at God—brought a big secret out into the open. Later, other kids admitted that they too felt that kind of anger but were usually afraid to talk about it. Maybe God wouldn't love them if God knew they were mad at him. Maybe God was punishing them for being bad kids by taking their parents away!

The counselor reassured the children that they were good kids and had a right to be angry. God was probably tough enough to take their anger and not punish them for it. Death is part of the natural process of living and dying, she told them, everything that lives must die. Death is not meant as a punishment. It just hurts to be without someone we love so much.

After the rest of the children had taken turns beating out their frustrations on one another (with foam bats only), David, Jason, and the others laughed and hugged until they all felt good again. It was such a relief to have all that pent-up anger released!

On other days, the kids pounded huge mounds of clay with their hands and eventually shaped them into "monsters." As the clay took form, the kids talked about how rage made them feel as if monsters lived inside of them, creating all kinds of anger that had to come out. Jason, David, and the others in the group discovered that using safe, creative ways to be angry gave them the means to express their feelings without destroying their families or themselves. They could release their intense emotions without getting themselves into trouble, which would only make them feel worse.

Jessica didn't like to talk about her feelings, so she rarely came to the Kids' Arts Group. She preferred putting her feelings into action her own way. One day, while her father was still alive, she asked her mother for a stamp. Jessica wanted to mail a letter she had written to the secretary of Health and Human Services in Washington, D.C. She had read a newspaper article about funding being cut for hospice care, the kind of care her father was receiving. She thought the government should know from a kid why the money was important.

Her father had been a lawyer and had taught his children the value of standing up for what they believe. Jessica was very proud of her effort. Two months later, when the secretary in Washington changed her mind and supported hospice care for the whole nation, Jessica knew she was part of the reason.

June 9, 1993

Dear Mrs. Hechsler,
You may not remember me, but I am the girl who tried to sell you a candy bar right in front of Star Market. I am ten years old and almost in sixth grade. I just finished my art lesson from Hospice. I am writing to you to talk about Hospice. Hospice

has been a great help to me during the last few months. My father, Jack G. Duncan, has had melanoma of the brain for a long time. He has cancer that cannot be cured. I was very upset because it was a shock on all of my family. I went to the hospital, and my father was half dead. He needed Mother. Mother was gone everyday at the hospital. I barely ever got to see him. He started to get better, and Hospice brought him home. He had to have eight-hour care through Shirley, a very nice lady that took Dad home and took care of him. Then my mother set us up with an art lesson. It is very good. We made costumes today. There are millions of people who need Hospice. You should know how it feels when a dying person in your family comes home. Please listen to me and support Hospice. Please!!

Sincerely,
Jessica Duncan

love in Christ

Months after his father died, David was bothered by nightmares of haunted houses, ghosts, and witches. Over and over again he drew the same picture—a haunted house filled with darkness and foreboding.

One day at the Kids' Arts Group, the counselor asked him to draw what the haunted house would look like if he got really close to it. This time he drew it with bats and bright lights in the windows and a huge dark gate in the middle. Then the counselor asked him to draw what it would look like if he walked through the gate of the house. Now all the darkness of the first drawings gave way to many colors and strong patterns that filled the paper, just as David's intense longings for his father were filling him.

While he drew, instead of feeling more frightened the closer he got to the inside of the house, David felt braver. "It's not so scary inside there after all," he said triumphantly. After the drawing series was completed, David was rarely bothered by the haunted house nightmare again.

Within a year of their father's death, the children's mother decided to marry a man whose wife had died of cancer and left him with

From a distance, David's haunted house is mostly dark.

Close up, the haunted house shows some light.

two teenage sons. The marriage meant a change of households for all five children, and each child worried about the new marriage in his or her own way. Jason would no longer be the big brother, and Jessica would be the only girl among three boys. David was afraid all the pets would not get along. Remarriage would also force their father into the past, as the grieving families combined to face the future together.

The dangers posed by these rapid changes were outweighed by the hope and love that urged the two families to become one. Still, for the children it was a lot to cope with. David, Jason, and Jessica made drawings of what the new family would look like. David's picture left out some of the people in the combined fam-

Inside, the haunted house is filled with intense patterns.

ilies, but included all of the pets of both, and his dead father, too, with arms shaped like an angel's wings.

Jason, Jessica, and David each reacted differently to the death of their father and grieved for him in his or her own way. In their family, it was as if three different fathers had died. Jessica had a different relationship with her father than Jason had with his dad. And David's way of being with his daddy was unique, also. Like brothers and sisters everywhere, they were rivals—sometimes competitors for attention and love, and sometimes competitors in grief. But their love and respect for one another ultimately held them together, even when they could not always share the others' feelings.

■ CREATIVE SURVIVAL STRATEGIES

What do you do when you are angry? Do you yell at your sister, push your brother, or strike the dog or cat? Does that help, or do you just feel bad and get into more trouble? What was the feeling that came over you just before you got angry? Can you describe it? Was it sadness? Fear? The next time you get mad, get a foam bat and try hitting a tree or a willing partner. The rules are: no hitting above the shoulders (to avoid hurting the face), and the hitting stops when *anyone* calls, "Time out!" Don't forget to yell out the name of who or what you are mad at and why! That's *really* important.

Or you can try using clay instead. Cut open a big plastic garbage bag and lay it flat on the floor. Then get a big chunk of soft clay (you can buy this from a pottery studio for very little money). Stand on a chair and throw the chunk on the plastic as hard as you can! Do it again. Yell and grunt when you do. Think of making big "cow pies" on someone's head with your clay. Do it over and over until you feel your anger is gone. Now perhaps you're ready to sit on the floor and quietly work the clay into a shape that feels good to you. Getting the anger out with bats or with clay will keep it from making you sick—giving you head-aches, stomachaches, or other pains. And it will keep you from hurting other people or yourself and getting into trouble. It's good to do these things with a partner. Who else in your family has a lot of anger stored up inside? Invite them to join you!

■ FURTHER EXPLORATIONS

Like Jessica's letter to the government, *Sadako*, a book by Eleanor Coerr, is a message of compassion to the powers that be. It is the story of a Japanese girl who loves to run, until she becomes sick with cancer. Her cancer is caused by the "bomb disease," the result of the radiation from two atomic bombs the United States dropped on Japan at the end of World War II. Sadako's anger and frustration at having leukemia and being stuck in a hospital are transformed into creativity and hope when a friend teaches her how to fold origami paper cranes. According to traditional myth, if she can fold a thousand paper cranes, her wish to live will come true. Sadako never finishes the thousand paper cranes, but her grieving classmates do after her death. Her story has become a cause for children around the world, who fold thousands of paper cranes every year and send them to Japan to be placed at the foot of her statue so that the world will remember never to bomb children again.

Niki & Angie

AGES FOUR AND TWO

AIDS and Suicide

Come on, Angie, you can do it!" cried four-and-a-half-year-old Niki. She was urging her little sister to walk. "Just follow the map! Walk right on it." Angie grinned at her sister, held out her arms, and sank to her knees. Then she crawled along the forty-foot length of narrow paper that Niki had made into a map of the two girls' world. Niki and the hospice counselor applauded anyway. It didn't matter that Angie was crawling, not walking. They were happy that she felt well enough to join their weekly art session.

Though Angie was only two years old, she had been infected with the AIDS virus since she was born. AIDS, which stands for Acquired Immunodeficiency Syndrome, is a disease that destroys the body's immune system. AIDS is thought to be caused by a virus that enters our bodies and grows within a kind of white blood cell. The various white blood cells of our immune system help us resist germs and get well from diseases. The virus kills one particular type of white blood cell, and eventually there are too few of this kind left to protect us. Then diseases can start to grow, making a person desperately sick with cancer or pneumonia or other infections that the body can normally defend itself against.

The virus believed to cause AIDS is called the human immunodeficiency virus, or HIV for short. People infected with the HIV virus, even if they don't yet show symptoms of AIDS, are said to be HIV positive.

Jennifer, Angie's mom, was infected with HIV, probably from a blood transfusion in the hospital. Because the virus was in her bloodstream when she was pregnant with Angie, she passed it on to her. The HIV virus is spread when bodily fluids from an infected person enter another person's bloodstream. This can happen through blood transfusions; by having sexual intercourse with an infected person; by sharing needles with a drug user who is in-

fected; or by having infected fluids enter the bloodstream in some
other way.

AIDS had ravaged both Jennifer's and Angie's immune systems.
Their bodies were plagued by many infections, leaving them nauseous and exhausted much of the time. The insides of their mouths
were so covered with sores it hurt to chew and swallow. As a
result, they grew very thin. Often they would be hospitalized
together, in the same room, to receive large doses of medications
and nutrition intravenously—that is, through their veins. These
transfusions helped their bodies fight the infections that attacked
them. For many months a thin tube ran through Angie's nose,
down her esophagus, and into her stomach. The other, free end
was taped to the back of her shirt. Several times a day, a large
syringe containing a rich formula of food and medicines was in-
serted into the taped end. This was the way Angie was fed when
she was too sore and weak to take food by mouth.

Angie's legs were too weak to support even her tiny body. It
was hard for her to grow, and she looked like a one-year-old
baby, even though she was two. Although she couldn't talk much,
she understood most of what was going on around her.

On this day, Angie seemed to feel pretty good. She scrambled
enthusiastically on all fours along the paper path to Niki's school,
Grandma's house, and the store. When Angie got to the drawing
of the big hospital, she grabbed a black marker lying nearby. She
scribbled all over the picture of the hospital building, muttering

words Niki couldn't understand. But Niki could tell Angie hated that hospital! Niki knew Angie and their mom had to go there every week, to have their blood checked and to see if any new infections had started in their bodies. Sometimes they didn't come home for days, or even weeks. Angie's thin arms were full of bruises and prick marks from all the shots and blood tests. Angie showed them to Niki as they both scribbled over that hated place on the map.

Their mom, Jennifer, watched the map play with a tired smile. She was having one of her bad days. There were very few days when both she and Angie felt well at the same time. The doctors had tried many different medications on Jen and Angie, but nothing seemed to help for very long. Today, Jen was weak from vomiting and diarrhea, the result of too much medicine and not enough food.

For more than a year now, Niki had been told by her mother, father, and grandparents that her mother and her younger sister were going to die of AIDS. But it hadn't happened yet, and Niki was young enough that it probably seemed to her they would just always be sick. She knew "to die" meant never to come back—the grown-ups had explained that to her. But Angie and her mother did keep coming back from the hospital.

Blood tests had shown that neither Niki nor her dad were HIV positive. Niki understood that to mean they didn't have the virus—or "buggies," as her grandmother called them—that made Jen and Angie so sick. Niki knew it wasn't her fault that her mom and sister were sick. And she knew she had to stay out of the bathroom when they were in there, and not touch their blood at any time, so she would stay healthy.

Angie crawled over to her blanket in front of the television and fell asleep, exhausted by the drawing and the play. The hospice counselor began rolling up the map, but Niki still had a lot of energy left. She started jumping around the living room. "It makes me tired just to watch her," said her mother. So the counselor took Niki out into the January snow piles to run around and have fun after all that thinking about the hospital.

Angie and her mom got a lot of care and attention from "Ma," Jen's mother, who came over every day to help out. They also got a lot of help from the hospice nurses and other relatives who came to the house to lend a hand. Niki was often left on her own. So the counselor was there especially for her, to give Niki the attention she needed. They had been working together for a month to help Niki cope with the daily changes and tragic losses that having both a mother and sister with AIDS would mean to her in the coming year.

The counselor had started by bringing Niki a big spiral-bound sketchbook, saying, "I know Angie and your mommy are really sick."

Niki had nodded.

"And I know you must have a lot of feelings about that."

"Right here," said Niki, patting her chest and nodding again.

"This book is for you to make a 'feelings book,' where you

can show all the different feelings you might have because Angie and your mom are so sick. It will help you to name the feelings as they come to you, so they don't scare you so much." Niki took the large book and leafed through the blank pages. She began to decorate the book with her name. She cut shapes out of colored paper and glued them onto the cover. Then the counselor drew four circles on the first page, and Niki thought of four feelings.

"My first feeling is happy!" she said with a glowing smile. She drew a smiling face in the first circle and labeled it "happy," with the counselor helping her spell the word. In the next circle she drew a face with big lollipop tears rolling down the cheeks. She asked the counselor, "What feeling do you think that is?"

"Oh! That face makes me very sad," the counselor answered.

"Right!" said Niki. "How do you spell 'sad'?" Niki wrote the letters for that feeling.

Then Niki growled and gave the counselor an angry look. She drew a face with jagged teeth clashing together. They labeled that one "mad." Niki drew the last face with huge eyes popping out and round, dark circles for the mouth and cheeks. She named that face "scared."

After Niki finished drawing and writing, she and the counselor practiced actually making these faces at each other. They talked about what made them feel each of these emotions. It was clear that Niki would have a lot of new and confusing feelings as she saw her mom and sister become covered with sores that wouldn't

Four faces that Niki drew for her feelings book.

heal, as they became too weak to get out of bed and eventually would lose the ability to talk to her. Learning to give words to her emotions would help Niki feel more in control of her life. It would lessen the feeling that things were just happening *to* her. For AIDS was also ravaging Niki, but in a different way.

Each week when the counselor arrived, she would ask Niki to get her feelings book. "Show me where you are today, Niki. Which feeling do you have?" Sometimes Niki could pick a face and name it, saying, "I have to go to the dentist tomorrow and I'm *scared*." Other days, she would move her finger all over the pages quickly, indicating that many feelings were assaulting her at once.

"Is there a new feeling that you want to add to your book

today, Niki?" the counselor would ask each time. "Brave" came right after "scared." Because, as Niki explained, "That's how you don't have to be scared at the dentist. You can be brave!" Shortly after she and Angie got new bunk beds in order to share a room together, Angie was hospitalized for two weeks, and "loneliness" went into the book. "Lonely," Niki said, "is lying in bed in a room all by yourself at night." Once, Niki asked how to spell "desperate," although she could not say what that feeling meant to her. The counselor and Niki went to ask her grandmother whether Niki might have heard that word used at home. Ma laughed and said, "Sure! Every morning when I arrive I tell Niki I'm *desperate* for a cup of coffee!" Niki laughed in agreement.

One day, Niki ran to meet the counselor with her book, shouting excitedly, "Do you know what's missing from my feelings book? 'Guilty'!" She was very proud of this word and started to draw it right away.

"Niki, how do you know the word 'guilty'?" asked the counselor.

But Niki couldn't say. She was too young to answer a question like that directly, to give an explanation. It was easier for her to choose from examples. So the counselor said, "Sometimes when I'm supposed to do something and I don't do it because I don't want to—I feel guilty." Niki shook her head. The counselor tried again. "You know, Niki, sometimes I feel guilty when my little boy does something wrong and I yell at him, and then he cries. Then I feel guilty!"

"Yeah! Sometimes my sister hits me and pinches me and pulls my hair, and then *she* feels guilty!" Niki seemed quite pleased with this example. But Angie was far too weak to do those things to Niki. It was more likely that Niki wanted to do those things to her sister. Angie received much more attention than Niki did, because Angie needed to be held and fed and washed by others just to stay alive. She was with their mother almost constantly. Because Angie was slowly dying, the adults wanted to be near her and comfort her. So Niki was left feeling jealous and angry, and then guilty for feeling this way.

Whenever Angie was home from the hospital and feeling well enough, she would join Niki and her counselor for an art project. Angie loved the colored markers, rubber letters, stamp pads, and stickers, just as any toddler would. It gave her a good feeling to use them all by herself. She could draw very intricate shapes and patterns that showed her age and intelligence, even if she couldn't walk or talk much.

One day, the counselor brought twenty-five pounds of clay to Niki and Angie's home. Angie got very excited and began stabbing the clay with pencils and scissors before the counselor could even get it out of the box. "Are you mad because you got stabbed at the hospital with needles?" the counselor asked her. Angie smiled and nodded and went right on gleefully gouging the clay. Niki joined her, chanting "Stab the doctor, stab the doctor," as they dug into the box. Both were glad to be on this side of the "injections."

In the spring, Angie started to have high fevers and uncontrollable infections that produced sores all over her face and body. Her tongue swelled and was covered with a thick white fungus called thrush. She could sip water only in a special way. Ma would make a pipette by putting a straw into a glass. Then she would cover the top of the straw with her finger and lift it out of the glass. The suction held the water in the straw while Ma moved it to Angie's lips. When she removed her finger, the water trickled into Angie's mouth, and Angie could drink without the hard surface of a plastic glass or even a paper cup or straw hurting her more. Jen was weak, too, so they both went back to the hospital. Everyone was afraid that this time Angie would die.

Because her family was at the hospital so much during that week, Niki stayed with a friend or relative every night. So the counselor went to see Niki at the preschool she attended. When Niki sat down to draw, she made a big face with tiny legs and drew jagged lines all around it, explaining, "This is fire. The baby is dying."

When the counselor asked what makes the fire, Niki refused to talk and threw her drawing at the counselor. Then she started to throw other things. The counselor showed Niki how to ball up tissues and bombard other people with them. Niki's intense feelings always broke through in outbursts of energy that needed safe avenues of expression. If these difficult feelings could pass through her without hurting her or anyone else, or being squelched by adults, then Niki could get relief from them.

After the tissue bombardment abated, the counselor asked Niki if she wanted to go outside to the playground and run off some energy. Niki headed for the door but stopped at the threshold. She looked back at the drawing lying on the floor.

"Is the drawing done, Niki? Is there something else it needs?" the counselor asked.

Niki went back to it and carefully added a loop from the top of the head to the top of the paper. "This is a rope, so God can take the baby up to heaven!" she said. Then she ran out the door.

But Angie didn't die that week. Someone else did.

Neither Niki nor her father, Doug, were HIV positive—they would not develop AIDS and die of it. But her father was very depressed watching his wife and baby in constant pain, wasting away day after day. It hurt him terribly to know he would lose them soon. He was also worried about how he could pay the enormous medical bills that were piling up. And he wondered what would happen to his car-repair business when people found out about the disease in his family. Doug had read newspaper stories about other families with AIDS. Those families were shunned and forced out of their homes and towns because people were ignorant and were afraid they would catch the deadly disease just by being near them.

Doug began to drink a lot of alcohol to make himself feel better about all these worries. But it didn't work. Instead, he felt more depressed and did dangerous things like driving when drunk.

One day, while Angie and Jennifer were in the hospital, Doug was at home waiting to meet with the minister of Ma's church. The minister had agreed to help the family make their AIDS story public by announcing it in church and then in the newspaper of their small town. The minister would organize a benefit celebration in the hope that they could get some financial support from the tightly knit rural community, where the whole family was well known.

But before the minister arrived, Niki's father went into his vegetable garden and shot himself in the head.

Relatives and hospice caregivers were shocked. They had been preparing for a death in Niki's family, but not this death. People were angry with Doug for abandoning his family just when they needed him the most. He knew his wife and daughter were going to die. How could he deliberately choose to leave Niki to survive alone?

Jennifer accepted her husband's death as a desperate act he was forced to take by the tragic circumstances they were all fighting. She explained, "I have a very strong attitude of 'Try me.' His whole attitude was 'Why me?' He danced as long as he could. The wind was just taken out of his sails. I feel bad for him. He didn't deserve that."

Jennifer had been able to stand up in Washington, D.C., and testify in the Senate, requesting help for people with AIDS. But even as she did that nationally, Doug had hidden their tragedy locally by telling the community that his wife had cancer and that they didn't know what was wrong with Angie. When the time came for the family to tell the truth and ask for help, he just couldn't face it.

Jennifer could not bring herself to explain the details of Doug's death to Niki, who wasn't yet five years old. Instead she told Niki that her daddy was dead because God had called him up to heaven to work on God's garden. It was very hard for Niki to believe that her daddy was suddenly gone. When the hospice counselor came to see the family on the day of his death, Niki was bouncing around cheerfully, exclaiming, "My daddy's dead! My daddy's dead!" She seemed unaware of the shocked silence of the adults watching her.

When Angie came home from the hospital the following week, she kept crawling around searching for her father. She would put his favorite magazine on his chair and wait for him to come home.

The counselor warned Jen and Ma that it was a mistake not to tell Niki the facts about her father's suicide. Once she got back to school, she would hear about it from other children. The story had been covered on television and in the newspapers. Teachers and parents were talking about AIDS now that it was clear there was a case in their own community. If her family didn't tell Niki the truth now, how could she trust what they told her in the future? But it was too painful for her mother and grandparents to reveal the whole truth to Niki. They felt she was too young to understand what they themselves didn't understand—how Doug could have abandoned them.

The day Niki went back to preschool after her father's funeral, a little boy came running up to her as she was getting out of the car. "Your daddy blew his brains out with a gun!" the boy shouted. Niki was stunned. She looked to her grandmother for help. "My . . . my daddy is working in God's garden. . . ." she said, a worried expression on her face.

For a month after her father's death, Niki was very upset; angry outbursts alternated with confused and sullen silences. She drew pictures of her father being pulled up into heaven by a rope and pictures of a gun hidden in a box. When she drew a picture with the caption "Gun Killing God!" her desperation was clear. She nearly tore up this drawing in a rage, but the counselor asked if she could show it to Niki's mother. Niki nodded and went off to watch a video with Angie.

Jen and Ma looked at the drawing. They could see that Niki needed to have her father's death explained to her. She was so confused by the bits and pieces she had heard that she was turning her anger against the God she had learned about in church and Sunday school, just when she needed God the most. She had a right to be angry about all the tragedy in her family, and she had a right to the truth. Only then could she begin to accept it in a way that could help her mourn what was happening in her life.

The counselor helped Jen and Ma explain Doug's death. They began with what Niki knew to be true through her own observations. "Niki, honey, you know how sad Daddy was about Mommy and Angie being sick?" her mother asked.

Niki nodded hard.

"And you know he started drinking alcohol again because he thought it would make him feel better. But it didn't, did it?"

Again Niki nodded.

"He just got more depressed and drank more. When people are depressed and drink a lot, they do foolish things. Your daddy did something really foolish—he played with a gun and it went off! It hit him right here." Jen pointed to the front of her head.

Niki nodded again, her eyes wide but calm. She climbed into her grandmother's lap, while her mother rubbed her back. "It wasn't your fault, honey. It wasn't anyone's fault. Your daddy loved you very much." Niki rested her head against Ma's chest as she took in this new information amidst loving reassurance. For now, it was enough for Niki to know that her dad had shot himself. When she was older and more able to understand that people have intense and conflicting emotions, she would realize that he chose to leave his family, even though he loved them. In the meantime, getting used to his death and absence was enough.

Two months later, Niki's grandfather called her counselor to say that Jennifer was having trouble breathing and she would probably die soon. Would she come and be with Niki? She arrived quickly to find Angie huddled under the dining-room table, sobbing and refusing to let anyone touch her. The counselor crawled under the table next to her and asked if she wanted to go see her mother. Angie nodded and let her favorite uncle carry her into the bedroom. She gestured toward the bed and lay down on top of her mother, crying softly for a few minutes. Then she held her arms up to be comforted by her uncle and her grandfather. After that, she wanted to go back to her mom, then return to the arms of her family. She was very sad, but as long as she was near her mother, she could be soothed.

Niki sat on the bed, kissed her mom, and was held by the gathering family. After a few minutes she grew restless, so the counselor took her outside to play with her cousins. Niki had just turned five, and she wanted to run and play. Children need physical release for the intense pressure they often feel from their emotions. Niki's desire to play didn't mean that she loved her mother any less.

Jennifer's breathing had been coming in short gasps, with longer and longer pauses of silence between each one. Her family wondered if each breath were her last. But then another deep barking sound would shatter the watchful, grieving silence. After forty-five minutes of this agonizing struggle, the hospice counselor, who had witnessed this painful process before, quietly spoke to Jen's brother. "You know, Jen may have trouble letting go and dying with all the family's love and strong feelings surrounding her and holding her here."

He agreed. So he asked each person to say his or her last farewell and take a break in the kitchen. Everyone seemed relieved to move around a little, and they left Jen to find her own peace.

Angie reached for the counselor, who was six months pregnant, and began to rub her belly. Ma and Niki joined Angie in the stroking, murmuring, "Love the baby, love the baby," as they cried, hugged each other, and touched the hope of new life in the presence of death.

Jennifer died a few minutes later, well loved by her parents, her children, her five brothers and sisters, and their families. All of them had helped take care of her. This time Niki got a chance to say good-bye. She understood that her beloved mother couldn't live any longer with the "buggies" inside of her, but she herself had been reassured many times that she would always be loved by her grandparents and the rest of the family.

Niki had a little bag woven in rainbow colors and filled with four beautiful stones. The hospice counselor had given it to her to rub whenever she felt worried. She wore it around her neck to her mother's funeral and held the worry stones tightly during the service. Later Niki, Angie, their cousins, and all the family carried huge purple balloons up to the cemetery on top of the hill where Jennifer was to be buried. As each person said a private good-bye to beautiful Jen, the balloons were released and rose high into the sky.

Jennifer had given custody of Angie and Niki to her parents, who lived nearby. The children tried to begin a new life with their grandparents, a life without their mom and dad. But Angie was getting weaker and sicker every day. She couldn't move on her own anymore and had to be carried everywhere. She had so many open sores on her body that it was painful for her to be held for very long. Curled into a little ball, Angie looked very sad. She clutched her Pooh Bear and sucked her pacifier constantly.

Angie missed her mother terribly. They had shared their illness together in the hospital and at home, and now she was too tired to fight AIDS alone. The doctors said the diarrhea Angie suffered from was her grief just pouring out of her. They had been able to stop it before, but now they could not. Angie spent many hours of every day nestled in her grandmother's comfortable lap, her tiny body and face made ancient by pain. The whole family cradled her in as much love and caring as they could create. Each time Niki made a drawing, she would make another for Angie, to try to bring a smile to her sister's sad face.

Angie was too weak to draw anymore, so the counselor brought her a "magic bag" of scrap materials to play with. As Angie pulled the pretty ribbons out one by one, a surprised smile broke through the agony in her little face. A delighted child still lived deep inside her.

Niki was very quiet during Angie's last week. With her counselor, she used clay to make many small balls—rolling each one between her hands until it was smooth. This repetition seemed to soothe her. Then she would place them one on top of the other, until she had built a huge mountain of clay balls. It seemed symbolic of all her individual problems adding up to one enormous obstacle. Niki didn't say much, except to check on the progress of her counselor's pregnancy and to murmur, "Love the baby." But she found comfort sitting in the laps of her counselor and her family.

Six weeks after her mother died, Angie too died peacefully at home, cared for by her sister, cousins, aunts, uncles, and grandparents. Again more purple balloons were launched from the cemetery. Niki made good-bye drawings and laid them on Angie's grave, right next to a Pooh Bear fashioned from flowers. Everyone wished Angie's spirit the peace and wellness she had never known in life. The air was filled with incredible sadness over Angie, Jen, and Doug—three funerals in four months. Yet there was also a feeling of relief. At least the dying was over.

But after so much trauma, how could Niki survive?

Niki, who was now in kindergarten, found it easy to make friends and to learn quickly. She was a bright child who endeared herself to her teachers and they took special care to let her talk openly about the death of her mom, dad, and sister.

Death was a big subject at show-and-tell, not just for Niki but for all the children. Inspired by Niki's stories, the kindergartners shared their tales of dead pets, grandparents, friends. All the kids were learning that every living thing eventually dies. And they were learning about AIDS together, too. The school counselors and the nurse told them that AIDS is a contagious disease but that you can get it only by introducing blood that is infected with the HIV virus into your own bloodstream. The children's knowledge helped take away their fears, and Niki was treated like all the other kids.

But the adults in her life still worried about how such a young child could grow up healthy and happy after so many losses. Her parents and her sister—her whole immediate family—had died within four months of one another. And AIDS and suicide are the hardest deaths for society to accept. People often feel that those who die from AIDS or suicide have done something wrong. What would happen as Niki got older and had more questions, maybe more anger? And what would happen if she rebelled by using alcohol or drugs? Who would help her? Her grandparents were facing retirement in a few years—what if something happened to them?

Niki was resilient because she had strong self-esteem. She was able to recover from the severe losses in her family because she knew she was loved. Every day, in different ways, she experienced the affection of those taking care of her. She knew she was good and that none of this tragedy was her fault. Her grandparents and others reminded her of these things every day. With hugs and praise and understanding, they let Niki know how much joy she brought to their lives.

Niki learned many ways to help herself. At night, when she had a bad dream, she got out her worry stones and whispered to them what was bothering her. Rubbing their smooth surfaces helped soothe her back to sleep. If she was very upset, Niki went into her grandparents' room for comfort. Niki continued to draw and write about her feelings, and she shared them with her family and teachers.

The counselor came to Niki's house once a week for a year after Niki's mother died. When an especially difficult question was bothering her, Niki would play ''school'' with the counselor. Using stuffed animals as puppets, they would take turns being the teacher or the student. After a few minutes of play, Niki felt safe enough to ask a hard question, like ''Why did my daddy die?'' or ''Why is there AIDS?''

Niki also learned more about the diseases of AIDS and alcoholism so she could better understand what had happened to her family. On school "Wellness Day," when there were special classes about the many ways to stay healthy, she and her grandmother visited a high school. They talked to the students about AIDS. Everyone made butterflies out of colored paper to send to Washington, D.C., for the first International Conference on Children and AIDS. Niki and her grandmother boarded the train for the capital carrying three boxes that contained two thousand butterflies from Vermont children. These butterflies were symbols of children all over the United States who had died of AIDS. They represented the compassion AIDS children and their families need and deserve, as well as the hope that someday a cure might be found.

In Washington, Niki's grandmother gave a speech about Angie to hundreds of people. Niki stood beside her on the podium. When she was asked, "What do you do when someone has

AIDS?" she bravely answered into the microphone, "You hug them!" The audience broke into thunderous applause.

Niki, her grandmother, and her counselor also worked on a panel in memory of Jennifer and Angie for the AIDS Memorial Quilt. The quilt project was begun in 1985 to make the nation aware that those who had died of AIDS were not just statistics of an incurable disease, but individuals who were loved and missed by friends and family members. The quilt was a graphic plea for medical and political action to stop the epidemic. And it offered a symbolic way to help individuals mourn their dead.

When the entire quilt with panels from all over the United States was assembled in 1993, it filled the Mall in Washington, D.C., all the way from the steps of the Capitol to the Washington Monument. Now so many people have died of AIDS—more than 225,000 in the United States by mid-1994—that the whole quilt, which continues to grow, may not fit together again in one place. But parts of it travel around the country to commemorate those who have died, to help their loved ones mourn their deaths, and to remind everyone of the need to prevent more deaths from AIDS.

The first step in making a panel is to choose a fabric for the background, measuring six feet by three feet. Then family and friends choose words and symbols representing their loved one, cut them from other materials, and sew them onto the panel. Then they add the name of the one who has died of AIDS. The panel is eventually sent to an AIDS regional headquarters, where it is attached to other panels from that part of the country.

The panel in honor of Jennifer and Angie was filled with their favorite things: an evergreen tree, which Jen felt was a symbol of health and strength; a Pooh Bear, which Angie loved dearly; and many purple balloons. At first Niki's grandmother didn't want to put in any symbol for Doug because she was still angry with him for "being a coward, and running away from his problems and abandoning his family." But later she realized that in a way he too was a victim of AIDS. The last piece she and Niki added to the panel was the image of a guitar that Doug used to play.

The panel took many hours of work, and other friends helped, too. As they sewed, they all explored memories of Jen and Angie, sharing these stories with Niki. When the panel was done and added to a hundred other panels, Niki could see she was not alone in having lost people she loved to AIDS. Connecting her family tragedy to a larger cultural problem gave her pain more meaning, and helped her symbolically join with other grieving children. This creative participation contributed powerfully to Niki's healing process.

Niki and Angie were unusually young to be the victims of two of the most difficult tragedies to understand in our world. But even the very young need to know the facts about complicated issues of life and death. Though children may appear to be "fine," untouched by or unaware of what is going on, they take in more than most adults around them realize.

Silent, unexpressed questions can torture the minds of children who suffer such enormous losses. "Did I make my mom sick? I brought home the chicken pox from school last week and she had to go to the hospital. Was it my fault?" "Was my mother angry with me for making my sister sick?" "Didn't my daddy want to be with me? Didn't he love me? Why did he leave me?" Even if a child can't speak these words, the questions need to be voiced and answered by those who survive to care for the child.

The more time and preparation you have to cope with a loss, the better you are able to make sense of it. Deaths that are sudden and inexplicable are the hardest for anyone to live with, particularly children. Niki's father's suicide will always be the more troubling death for Niki to understand as she grows. AIDS is the tragedy she has the most control over, through her knowledge of the disease and its prevention, and through the care and love she was able to give her mother and sister.

■ CREATIVE SURVIVAL STRATEGIES

Make a "feelings book" in your journal by drawing faces that show different expressions. Name the expressions. See how many emotions you can come up with. When does each feeling happen to you? How do you move from one feeling to another? Do you ever have more than one feeling at a time? How can you recognize your feelings as they come, and let go of them, without acting on every one of them? Is there something you can learn from your feelings? Each emotion is valuable because it is your own. It is important to experience a variety of emotions. This will prevent you from becoming stuck with a single feeling until it becomes destructive. And experiencing many different emotions is part of enjoying the richness of life—your own life!

Collect some "worry stones" that feel good in your hand. Find a special bag or box for them and keep them near you. Use them when you are feeling worried about someone or something that is affecting you. Or make your own "trouble dolls." Start with pipe cleaners cut into two-inch pieces. Wrap one piece around the middle of a second piece to make a "T" shape; this gives you the arms and body. Next, glue a small wooden bead with a hole in it onto the top of the pipe cleaner T for the head. You can draw in a face, then glue on small pieces of embroidery floss or thread for hair. Use different colors of the floss or thread to wrap around the body and arms, over and over again, to make the clothing. Tie a knot and cut the string short, and put a dot of glue on the knot to keep it from unraveling. Now you have your first trouble doll. Make others with different expressions and colors for your different feelings. Keep the dolls in a small box under your pillow or near your bed, and tell each one a trouble you have when you can't sleep. Try to imagine what the dolls might say to help you feel better. The dolls don't mind hearing your feelings *whatever* they are; they will "work on your worries," carrying them out of your mind while you sleep.

■ FURTHER EXPLORATIONS

There is a short book about AIDS called *Losing Uncle Tim*, by MaryKate Jordan, which is beautifully illustrated by Judith Friedman. A boy named Daniel has an uncle with AIDS, and the antique toys and checker games they share must come to an end, as Daniel struggles with his feelings and fears.

AIDS: You Can't Catch It Holding Hands, by Niki de Saint Phalle, is also illustrated and explains in simple terms the basics about AIDS. It covers testing for AIDS and controlling the spread of the disease, and explores its impact on young people experimenting with sex and love.

School Days

The Death of Friends

It seemed like any other school morning. Four-and-a-half-year-old Molly and her older brother and sister were standing on the side of the busy country highway waiting for the bus to take them to school. They were restless and mischievous and unsupervised—laughing, pushing, racing around one another.

Finally they glimpsed the front of the huge yellow bus as it lumbered along the highway behind a truck. From a nearby yard, a dog suddenly ran out into the road. Molly saw the danger and chased after it. Truck brakes squealed and tires burned as the big rig tried to stop. There wasn't enough time. Although the dog escaped, Molly bounced off the front end of the truck and flew fifty feet into the air, landing in a silent heap at the side of the road.

Her brother and sister watched in horror, then began to scream. The truck skidded to a stop, and the bus pulled up behind it. Both drivers dashed out to help Molly. Inside the bus, children pressed against the windows, trying to see who had been hit. Shocked and silent, they watched as the men huddled over the little girl's limp body. People came running from the general store up the road and tried to comfort her screaming brother and sister.

It seemed to take forever for the state police and the ambulance to arrive. By then, the children on the bus knew that Molly was the one who had been hit and that she was dead. A neighbor from the general store drove her brother and sister home; the rest of the children went on in the bus. By ten o'clock, everyone in the country school had heard what had happened that morning. From kindergarten through senior high, kids, teachers, and staff were all affected. Some were crying, some sat on the floor stunned, others held each other.

The principal immediately called the county crisis team. They came that afternoon to talk to the children who had been on the bus and were obviously most upset. But how could strangers comfort these terrified kids who had seen an accident that caused a little girl to fly into the air and be killed?

The principal organized a brief memorial service for Molly. It took place in the gym the next morning. Students and teachers listened as their principal stood before them and acknowledged the sadness, fear, and shock that each might be feeling. Molly's music teacher sang a song she had composed for her. Molly's pre-K teacher read a poem that the other children in Molly's class had helped to write.

After several days, the principal could see that many teachers and students were still upset despite the visit of the crisis team and the memorial service. So he asked a hospice counselor to speak with his staff and to run a support group for any children in the school who wanted to attend.

He told the counselor that rumors were flying. The driver was on drugs. . . . The truck had deliberately sped up when Molly ran into the road. . . . Someone pushed her into the road. . . . The kids were playing "chicken" and trying to dodge vehicles. The principal himself was angry with the parents for not supervising their children at the bus stop; he had asked them to do so in the past. It seemed everyone was looking for someone on whom to blame the terrible accident, a tragedy that should never have happened. Worried parents were calling the school. Teachers, sad and angry themselves, were unable to talk with the students. They didn't know what to say. And the kids were too scared and upset even to pretend they could pay much attention to their schoolwork.

A week after the accident, the counselor arrived to meet with the teachers and staff. The meeting was supposed to be held in the school library at the end of the day, but no one showed up. Some of the teachers were apparently tired of dealing with the situation and felt resentful of outside help. Many found the whole incident too painful to discuss. So over the loudspeaker the principal had to order the staff to "come now" for the meeting on "Children and Death." When the thirty adults finally began to trickle into the big room, they sat as close to the door and as far away from the hospice counselor as possible. They were afraid to get any closer to this frightening situation than they already had.

The counselor introduced herself by telling a few stories about other children and teachers she had worked with who had faced the death of a child. Then she tried to find out what most troubled the teachers and staff about Molly's death. Some felt that school wasn't the place for dealing with death. They wanted to let families handle this subject on their own, at home. Others wanted to help themselves and their students cope with the trauma, but had no idea how to go about it. And everyone was confused about the facts—about what had really happened that morning at the bus stop. The teachers and staff finally agreed that what they needed first of all was accurate information about the accident. Then there could be an opportunity for the adults to express their feelings and the children theirs. Finally they could all work together to give one another reassurance that life would get back to normal and once again be safe for everyone at school.

The counselor explored the teachers' memories of other deaths in their lives. She wanted to see how Molly's accident brought up past painful times for them. She pointed out that these disturbing feelings might prevent the teachers from helping their students now. Many teachers were also afraid they would break down in front of the kids, that they would upset their students more by crying. The counselor told them that crying in front of their students would do no harm. In fact, it would be good for the kids because it would show them that each child is important, that each child would be missed and mourned if he or she died. The kids needed to see that teachers and staff cared, too. It would show the students that they could trust their feelings to these caring teachers.

"What should be done about Molly's papers and desk?" one teacher asked. The counselor said not to remove them for now, that it was important to leave Molly's artwork on the walls and keep her desk in its place for a while. It would be a mistake to suggest that Molly had not been a member of the pre-K class or that she could be quickly forgotten. This would frighten the children almost more than her actual death. After a few weeks the children could be told that their class would never be the same without Molly, but that it was time to move on. The whole room could be rearranged and the walls redecorated, as a symbol of giving everyone a fresh start. Meanwhile, she advised them to keep the daily routine of the classroom the same as it was before Molly's death. The kids could depend on this stability to feel safe. Through it they could learn that even after a tragedy, life goes on.

Following the meeting, the principal agreed to create a statement that would be read first thing the next morning to every child in the school. Then it would be sent home. It was important that this message be read aloud in the classrooms by trusted teachers and not come over the loudspeaker. That way, students could ask questions and have a chance to be heard. The statement included the facts of the accident—that Molly had run into the road after a dog and that the truck driver had tried to stop in time but could not. Next came information about what the police had done to follow up the details of the accident—measured skid marks, tested the driver's blood and found no illegal substances in him or in the truck. The statement then explained what would be done in the future to keep children safe at their bus stops—parents would take turns supervising each bus stop. Finally, the principal's message acknowledged the different kinds of feelings people might have in response to Molly's death: anger, guilt, sadness, fear, worry, shame, relief, or other emotions. The principal said it depended on whether you knew Molly or her family, or had experienced another death in your own life. The message acknowledged you might not feel very affected at all, and that was okay, too.

The statement also said that classes would go on as usual. However, on Thursday mornings there would be a special support group for anyone who wanted to leave class and get together to do activities with a counselor. Parents' permission was needed for this. Finally, the message announced that plans would be made for creating a memorial for Molly on the playground. The children would be asked for their ideas and participation.

The next Thursday morning the support group began for children who felt troubled by Molly's death—or by any other loss that the accident had brought up for them. When the counselor from the hospice arrived lugging her bags of art supplies, the school guidance counselor took her to the cafeteria. There was a space for the group of eighteen kids at a table in the corner. The guidance counselor deposited the hospice counselor in this noisy, public place, and then never looked in on the group again. It was clear to the hospice counselor that he wanted nothing more to do with the matter. Fortunately, three parents had accompanied their children to the group, and they were willing to help out.

The youngest child in the group was four and a half—a classmate of Molly's. The oldest was fourteen and had seen the accident from the bus. Molly's parents had not allowed her brother and sister to come to the group, because the parents didn't want them discussing the accident. They were afraid the police and social service authorities might take the children away from them for neglect. Problems with lack of parental supervision had arisen in that family before. As the group sat down to draw with markers, everyone was nervous.

The counselor began by telling the kids that her brother had been killed in an accident involving a truck, so she knew a little of what they might be feeling. She said that it helps to get your feelings out onto paper and into words. That way your feelings don't give you stomachaches and headaches, or make you so angry that you get into trouble or get scared by what's inside you.

The counselor asked them to draw a personal experience of being lost or losing something. The kids recalled how their dogs were killed, or when their grandmothers had died, or how their dads had moved away and left them when their parents were divorced. One girl drew a picture of the house fire that had killed her aunt. Another drew a car accident that had killed her father. A boy drew himself stuck in an elevator, unable to reach the buttons. They talked about how these memories and feelings of being alone, lost, scared, and helpless had come back in the days and nights since Molly died.

After the drawings were discussed, some of the children began to cry because of their feelings and memories. The counselor suggested that the kids stand very close together in a big circle and hold hands. Then she taught them the Squeeze Game. Four squeezes along with the words "Do you love me?" Three squeezes with the three words "Yes, I do!" Two squeezes and the two words "How much?" "SQUEEZE!!" By the end of the Squeeze Game there was a feeling of reassurance among the group and even some smiles. When the counselor left the school a while later, she saw some of the kids from the group teaching the Squeeze Game to Molly's brother and sister. "This is what you do when you get scared about Molly. . . . See, hold onto me and squeeze my hand. . . ."

The next Thursday, the counselor brought a puppet-show video for the group. It was about two friends who saw another friend get hit by a car. While the kids in the group watched, they created puppets out of paper bags and scraps of material. It made them more comfortable to be active as they listened to the sad story. Afterward the children's puppets talked about their intense feelings—of being scared and feeling guilty that they had not stopped Molly, not stopped the truck, or had not died themselves.

For the third session the counselor brought a big box of clay and a large plastic sheet that she put down on the floor. Then everyone took about two fistfuls of dark red clay and began throwing them onto the floor to make the clay smooth. With each big *splat* that the clay made, the kids said what they were mad about. "Aren't you mad that Molly died?" "Yeah, yeah!" *Splat*. "What else are you mad about?" the counselor coached them. The answers ranged from parents not being at the bus stop, to the truck driver not stopping in time, to God for letting it happen. *Splat! Splat!! Splat!!!*

For the time being, the kids had pounded out their anger. They sat down to model the clay into whatever shapes they wanted. There were memorials and monsters, flowers and coffins. Afterward, they all took more clay home, with instructions to use it (with their parents' permission) as a way to be angry but safe at the same time. They could pound away at the clay instead of striking out at their sisters, brothers, parents, pets, or even possibly hurting themselves.

At the last session, the kids made little memorial candles and holders. Then they created a ceremony to say good-bye to Molly, to other family and friends they had lost, and to each other in the group. The session finished with the Squeeze Game and lots of hugs. It was hard to end, but the students knew that endings were what this group was about. Finding ways to understand what had happened, exploring their feelings of loss, and memorializing these losses through drawings, symbols, and rituals helped every-one say good-bye to Molly.

As the last step in the mourning process, the group gave them-selves permission to continue their lives without guilt. The coun-selor told them it was okay to have fun, to run and play, to love other people. You know you still care about those who have died, even though you are done crying for now. So the students and counselor hugged and squeezed hands again and gave one another permission to go on.

■ ■ ■

Another school faced a different crisis when the principal and teachers learned that a twelve-year-old student was not going to live much longer. Catherine had been ill with a very rare liver cancer for two years. The chemotherapy that had reduced the size of her tumor twice before was not working this time. Her liver could no longer clean the waste products out of her body. The small, thin face that peeked out from under Catherine's baseball hat was now yellowish gray. In the last month, her belly had become so swollen that it was hard for her to stand and walk. So she no longer came to school.

Even though everyone had known for a long time that Catherine was seriously ill, this new reality was a shock to the middle school where she was in the sixth grade. The only good thing about it was that teachers, staff, and students had a little time to prepare for Catherine's death.

The staff began to plan how the children could best be told that Catherine would die. They knew they could not help the students through this painful process without first having a chance to talk about their own feelings. Then, from that, they could formulate a plan to help their students deal with this painful situation. So they asked a hospice counselor to come help them all find ways to say good-bye.

Catherine had been in the hospital for several weeks and now was being moved home to die. The hospice counselor suggested that the school guidance counselor call her family for a report on how she was doing, and then update it everyday. Did Catherine want classmates or teachers to visit her? Would messages be better? What help did the family need? Her teachers feared that on the actual day of her death, whenever that might be, they would be quite upset. They were not sure they could teach without help. So substitute teachers, familiar to the students, were hired to give extra support.

The principal agreed to put the information from the family in an honest but gentle message. The message would go to every staff member and be read to every student by their homeroom teachers, with updates following frequently. This was the first message:

As many of you may know, Catherine Street, a sixth grader in Mrs. Darcy's class, has been sick with a rare form of liver cancer for two years. She has been in the hospital for several weeks, but the doctors fear she will die soon because the medicines are no longer working and there are no more to try.

Catherine is feeling very weak now, but she plans to come home today. She won't be coming back to school again. Her friends and classmates are invited to stop by the guidance office and make good-bye cards to send to her. A special journal will also go back and forth between Catherine's house and the school, so she can send messages, too.

Please remember to be extra kind and gentle with each other and other members of Catherine's family during this sad time. Mrs. Roy, the guidance counselor, will stay after school every day for anyone who wants to talk. We will keep the gym open after hours so that anyone who wants to work off their energy may do so. I will be giving you updated news about Catherine every few days. Please feel free to come to me or Mrs. Roy or your teachers with any thoughts or questions that this bad news brings up for you. Thank you.

Two weeks later Catherine died. Teachers read the students an-other message from the principal that described her death as peace-ful and free of pain thanks to the medications she was taking. She was surrounded by her loving family, favorite stuffed ani-mals, and the students' cards and drawings. Anyone who wanted time out to talk with the guidance counselor was invited to come to the library conference room anytime during the day. A photograph of Catherine had been put on the front bulletin board with the words "We love you, Catherine!" The principal added that the funeral would be in a small church at night, but the school would offer a memorial service after classes on Fri-day for anyone who wanted to come. Children who wanted to help create the service could join the counselor after school all week.

The staff were surprised by the enthusiasm and variety of ideas with which ten students planned the memorial service. They made a huge cloth banner with "CATHERINE" spelled in cutout letters. They decorated it with fabric flowers and musical notes, her fa-vorite things. It was hung between the posts that supported the large outdoor tent where the service was to be held. Then the planners chose their favorite songs from class for everyone to sing together. Three children picked out poems to read that they knew Catherine had liked. They wrote it all up in a program, which they decorated, so people would have something to hold in their nervous hands when they came to the service.

Her classmates made a photo-and-drawing collage of Catherine at school, at home, and in the hospital, to display at the service. Their last task was to gather wildflowers from the school grounds right before the service began. These were used to decorate the tent. The only thing the staff had to do was to make sure the students had the supplies they needed for the banner and collage.

At the beginning of the service, the principal gave a brief welcoming speech. Then the children took over. They decided to end the half-hour service with all two hundred people standing in a giant circle, holding hands. They sang "Amazing Grace" and then said good-bye to Catherine with the Squeeze Game. The hospice counselor had taught the kids the game while they made the banner. Everyone cried, but there were smiles and hugs and a lot of healing, too, for children, staff, and parents alike.

．　■　■

Perhaps the hardest death for family and friends to understand is the suicide of a child.

Jackie was only fifteen years old when she hanged herself in her barn. It seemed no one had known she was even thinking of taking her life. Sure, she had lots of problems—changing friends suddenly, getting bad grades, doing drugs, missing basketball practices and games. In the six months before her death, everyone had tried to help—her guidance counselor, basketball coach, teachers, and old friends. But she resisted each attempt to reach out to her. She quit the basketball team, ignored concerned teachers, dropped her friends, and took up with a boy who used drugs.

The old friends she left behind were stunned by her death. They were filled with disbelief, hurt, guilt, and fear. Because it was summertime, school wasn't open to offer support. So the kids drifted from one home to another, from street corners to the wake and funeral, and back home again. The rumors were as violent as Jackie's death. She was pregnant. . . . She was still alive when they cut the noose from her neck. . . . She had needle tracks on her arms . . . on and on. If it could happen to Jackie, who was so strong, so funny and smart, so daring, it could happen again to any of them.

At the request of the parents' of Jackie's friends, a male social worker and a female hospice counselor offered to start a support group. It would meet one evening a week for a month. Eight kids who had attended school with Jackie from kindergarten through sixth grade (when she had changed schools) came to the group.

The counselors were concerned that no one would want to speak up at the first session, so they arrived with a lot of questions planned. They didn't have a chance to ask many because the kids just couldn't stop talking about what had happened to Jackie. Most of the talk was trying to sort out the rumors. "I heard she was still alive when they cut her down, and they could have saved her if they had tried. . . . I heard she was five months pregnant! . . . I heard her head was smashed where someone hit her. . . . I heard she had needle tracks on her arms from heroin!"

The counselors had come prepared with the facts from the family, the police, and the autopsy. So they were able to put the false

rumors to rest. Blood tests showed that Jackie was neither pregnant nor had drugs in her system. Death was by strangulation and
was instantaneous. She had a bruise on her head where she hit the
side of the barn door when she jumped off the chair.

The kids relaxed a little and began to talk about all the things
they had done together over the years. School projects, parties,
camping trips, sports events, pranks they pulled on one another
—all were recollected and shared. "Remember the time she cut
Debbie's hair? That was the last sleep-over Debbie ever came
to!" They laughed and they cried. They were all so alike, all these
friends—how could Jackie have done this thing? The unspoken
implication was, "If we were so alike, how could she be dead and
I still be alive? If she couldn't stop herself, how could I? Could I
kill myself, too?" But nobody said those words out loud the first
evening. The question was too terrifying.

The second session focused on losses the kids had known personally, like divorce or illness or other deaths. It turned out that
half of them were from divorced homes. Half of them also had a
mother who had died or was suffering from cancer. Many of them
were adopted as well. The counselors had expected to hear that
the kids had losses in their lives. Nevertheless, the multiplicity and
intensity of these experiences surprised them. All the losses had
left the kids in the group particularly vulnerable to Jackie's tragedy
and in need of extra support. Perhaps that was why they had come.

The kids explored the differences between how divorce made

them feel and how they reacted to death. One said, "Separation is so messy—all the time the rules are changing. . . . Who gets what, who gets me. . . . Now they are making me choose between vacationing in Texas with my father or in Vermont with my mother! Why do they put me in this position?! It's so *hard*. . . ." But Jackie's death was so *final*. There were no choices. The only decision each one had to make was how to live with the memories, how to make sense of her death.

The third time the group got together, the counselors brought a huge, twenty-five-pound block of clay for everyone to jab, smash, twist, and physically work out all the feelings that Jackie's death created inside of them. Unlike small children, who need guided activities in order to express their feelings, teenagers generally prefer to talk. Language is their primary creative medium. Still, the counselors offered other materials, such as the clay, colored markers, paper, rocks, crystals, and shells, as accompaniment to their verbal explorations.

But the clay was particularly useful to the teenagers. With it they could express all the frustration and anger they felt at not being able to help Jackie and keep her alive. As the kids twisted and smoothed the clay, the counselors reminded them that no one can keep another person alive once he or she has made a final decision to die. You can try to help, to let someone know you love and value them. You can tell them there is hope and professional help available. And you can inform other adults about the situation. Yes, you can be a great friend, but the responsibility for whether your friend lives or dies is not yours to shoulder. Ultimately, it is not your choice to make.

The last session arrived. Still none of the kids had ever mentioned considering suicide. The counselors knew they had to bring this up, to find out if anyone else was at risk. Surely the kids had thought about the possibility for themselves. When someone old or sick dies, it reinforces the idea that you have to be old or sick to die. But when a healthy young friend dies, it means "I can die, too." The counselors needed to find ways to support these teenagers so they would not choose that terrible escape.

But when the social worker asked the group if anyone had ever thought about committing suicide, there was silence. The kids looked at their hands; no one would speak. Finally he said, "You know, when I was depressed and discouraged about my life, I thought about killing myself, about taking this final way out. Everyone has thoughts like these at some time or other. We get overwhelmed with suppressed feelings of anger and rage, or we feel frustrated and ignored, or we want to hurt others by hurting ourselves. But these feelings come and they go. It doesn't mean you will act on them. I'm still alive!"

The kids shifted in their seats and looked at one another but still didn't speak. Then the hospice counselor said essentially the same thing about herself. Little sighs of relief went around the room, little nods of the head, but still no words.

The counselor went on, "You *have* thought about it, but you are *not dead!* Why not? What happened after your first thought? What came next?" One by one, the kids reluctantly admitted that their next thought had been to choose a method of killing themselves. One girl said, "I thought about running the car into the wall, but I don't know how to drive yet." Another confessed, "Since my mom got cancer, there are enough pills in my house to kill anyone. But then she'd have to fight the disease alone." A third said, "I thought about the kitchen knives or the gas in the oven, but how could I cut or poison or hurt in any way *this body?* I just couldn't do that to *me!*" Each of these kids had a strong sense of being whole, of being connected to other people. This sense of being "intact" kept them from going further in thinking about hurting themselves.

But other members of the group had not shied away from the idea of suicide. They had decided on a way of killing themselves. And they looked worried and guilty.

"So what happened next? You chose a way to kill yourself, but you are *not dead.* What kept you from going ahead with it? What did you do next?" These kids agreed that the next thing they tended to do was make a mental list. On one side were the people who would be upset if they died; and on the other side were those who would not care. Most of the kids found the list reassuring. It reminded them of the love they knew was in their lives. Perhaps they had forgotten to notice it. Or perhaps their frustrated parents had forgotten to show their teenagers just how much they meant to them.

But there was one girl in the group who found the list very depressing. It did not make her want to choose life. "Which side of the list would Mom be on? She's always so mad at me. And what about Dad? He's not even here to care anymore!" She admitted her next thought was to imagine her own funeral and wonder who would come. Suddenly she blurted out, "I want to know—if I died would they turn off all the traffic lights? Would this town *stop* for the day? Would everyone say, 'Michelle is gone—our town feels empty today.' Would they?"

Her anguish and unanswered questions clearly showed that Michelle was still undecided about living out her life. She was in danger. The group tried to reassure Michelle that she was valued; each person told her how much they liked her, what they admired about her, and why they needed her as a friend. Her life was important to them even if her father had abandoned his family and her mother was angry all the time, even if the entire town couldn't show her appreciation. They understood that she was looking for something to signal her value in this world, and they tried to provide that. Michelle looked surprised at this outpouring from her friends. She looked at each person, questioning them—"Is that really true? Do you really think so?" She sank back in her seat to consider these things.

The counselors knew one session of reassurance would not be enough to keep a distraught teenager from suicide. But it was a good start. They would talk with her parents as well, to make a plan of support with Michelle and her family.

When the group began, the counselors had said that the last session would end with a symbolic ceremony. It would be a chance to burn any feelings the kids wanted to be rid of. They would write their thoughts down on paper, put them into a cauldron, and then set fire to the paper words. It was a good way to clean out regrets, angers, and guilt, such as "I should have kept calling Jackie, trying to still be her friend. . . ." "If only I had told her how much I loved her and admired her. . . ." "What if she had come to my party. . . ." Listening to sad, quiet music in the dark, with candles burning, the kids wrote their private messages. They knew they didn't have to share them with anyone, so they could write what they truly felt.

When it came time to throw them into the pot, Michelle slowly pulled a stack of letters from her purse. As the group watched the flames devour all their notes of pain and remorse, she said, "I've been thinking about this burning ceremony, and I brought all the letters I've gotten from a friend at camp for the last two years. They're all about suicide, our fantasies and plans. But I've decided that this is not a good way to live anymore!" She took a deep breath and dropped them in the cauldron. The group congratulated her wisdom and strength. Being able to burn the suicide letters was a sign of change Michelle had been looking for, and it came from within. After she spoke, the kids held candles and stood in a circle. A flame was passed from one candle to the other, in honor of Jackie. They all said their last silent good-byes to the friend who had chosen to leave.

The last thing the counselors asked the kids was "What should we tell your parents about how to prevent teenage suicide? They want to know how to help." Everyone shrugged or shook their heads, overwhelmed with the recent memory of Jackie's death. "You *can't* prevent it!" someone said. But the counselor replied, "No! Listen to yourselves—those steps you went through. You taught us that you need to know on which side of the list the people in your lives belong. Maybe you need more hugs and reassurances. Maybe you need to hear 'I love you!' even when you are being your most prickly, obnoxious selves!"

Everyone laughed, looking a little relieved. "Yeah, you can tell them that!" The group ended with their own hugs and thanks for all that they had shared and taught one another about surviving suicide.

Because this group took place in a small town, the kids often ran into the hospice counselor, who lived there, too. This was a great source of embarrassment to the group members. Usually they would cross the street to avoid encountering her. The counselor knew not to take it personally. She had seen them cry, rage, and give voice to their worst fears. She represented grief, pain, and the kids' own vulnerability. Nobody wanted to confront that on a public street.

One girl in particular, named Kim, passed the counselor regularly at the supermarket, the library, or in front of city hall. Each time she was clearly mortified. Once, while standing in line at the grocery store, Kim's sister asked her who "that person" was. Kim whispered a response that produced raised eyebrows, a second look, and a quick escape for both of them.

But one day, two months after the last session, the counselor was walking with a colleague along a crowded street at lunchtime. She saw Kim coming toward her with a friend. Anticipating Kim's embarrassment, the counselor prepared to make the encounter easy. But this time Kim came right up to her and grabbed her arm. "Do you know what *today* is?" Kim asked. "It's Jackie's *birthday!* She would have been *sixteen* years old today!"

The counselor was amazed by the contact and wanted to hold Kim there for a minute. But she didn't want to say anything too personal in front of her colleague or Kim's friend. So she simply asked, "What did you used to do for her birthday?"

Kim thought for a minute, then burst out laughing. "We used to play *freeze your underwear!*" The counselor was surprised. Her colleague looked shocked. Kim's friend rolled her eyes and giggled.

"I've never played Freeze Your Underwear," the counselor replied. "How do you play it?"

"Well, we would all go to Jackie's house for an overnight party. And the first one to fall asleep—you take their underwear and put it in the freezer. Then when she wakes up in the morning, she has to put it on while everyone watches!" They all started laughing and shivering at the bizarre image. Then Kim waved good-bye and trotted off with her friend.

The colleague looked at the counselor, grinning doubtfully. "What was that all about?"

"You see," said the counselor. "*That* is why adults think that teenagers don't grieve. Because they do it in their own way, with gross stories and a crazy sense of humor."

For children and teenagers there is a big difference between the death of an adult and the death of a friend. When old people die, it seems normal, if sad. Old people are supposed to die. Even parents die sometimes. But kids aren't suppose to die—their lives are just getting started. For kids who survive the death of a close friend, this death means something new: If my friend dies, that means I can die, too! I feel guilty and responsible for not dying. Did I make my friend's death happen? What *did* happen? Will it happen again? How will you keep me safe? If I did die, would it matter? Who would care? How can you show me that the life of each person is important?

Sometimes these questions will find an adolescent's voice to ask them out loud. Sometimes they will be asked only with the silent eyes of a grieving child. Whether the questions are spoken or not, it is vital that children and teenagers get answers to them—with honesty, understanding, and acts of reassurance.

To cope with emotional pain, kids use every resource and skill they have. That includes humor. Dead ducks and roadkill stories, bawdy jokes and funny memories, such things allow kids to gain a distance from death. At the same time, their humor keeps the issues of death and danger before them. Their humor allows them to be who and what they are.

■ CREATIVE SURVIVAL STRATEGIES

Perhaps there are some feelings you would like to be rid of—to burn away. Get some paper and a pen. Listen to your favorite quiet music and think about whom you have lost in your life. What are the difficult feelings you have? What makes you feel guilty or angry or confused? Can you put them into words and burn them? Can you let the fire really take those feelings away, so you don't have to go on living with them? Maybe the words can start with "If only I had . . ." "I was really mad when . . ." "I'm sorry about the time I . . ." This can be a way to forgive yourself for being human and making mistakes. Everyone makes mistakes with friends, with oneself. No one is perfect. Let your grief be sad and full of memories, but don't punish yourself by living with blame and regrets.

Find a special but safe place meant for burning things—a metal pot or a fireplace or a bonfire outside will do. Then ask an adult to help you light the fire. Be *sure* you do not try this on your own. Closely watch it so that the papers and feelings can burn in safety. You can keep your messages private or share them if you wish. As you watch the flames, there will be very little smoke because paper burns quickly, so you will be able to take lots of deep breaths and clean out your insides. When the ashes cool, you can find a garden and put the ashes there so your grief will help something else to grow. Later, if these feelings come back, you can burn them again. You may need several fires to purge them, especially if you have been carrying them around inside of you for a long time. This ancient ritual has been used in all cultures in one form or another. So by using it you join an age-old human tradition, participating in the pattern of life and death and renewal on Earth.

■ FURTHER EXPLORATIONS

Though they compete against each other, a boy and girl learn to be friends and create an imaginary world to share. But one of them must learn to survive terrible grief when the other is killed in *Bridge to Terabithia*, by Katherine Paterson. How their special world can be transformed from a place of sorrow and pain into a source of healing completes this powerful story.

Teen Suicide, by Janet Kolehmainen and Sandra Handwerk, is a good introduction for friends and family of potential and completed suicide victims. It reviews warning signs and myths, and offers profiles of six teenagers affected by suicide.

Shelly & Bobby

Murder

Shelly gazed out the car window at the last of the spring snow as her mother drove slowly through the woods near their old house. Bobby, Shelly's two-year-old brother, was singing to himself in the backseat. He seemed happy to be going for a ride. But Shelly's stomach felt tight with dread. She tried to let the sight of the familiar trees relax her. They hadn't been back for four months, not since her mother had packed up their things and taken eight-year-old Shelly and her brother out of the house and away from their father. Her mother had decided it would never be safe to go back, and she had filed for divorce.

The fighting had been going on ever since Shelly could remember. Her father would get angry and start yelling at everyone. That would lead to his pounding his fist on the table so hard it made the plates jump. Shelly had learned to get out of the room at that point, to take Bobby with her and hide as quickly as possible. But even from her hiding place she could always hear the terrible sound of her mother pleading and then her father's powerful hand slapping her mom. Over and over. Finally the front door would slam. When Shelly was sure her father had left, she would creep down to the kitchen, put Bobby in the high chair, and give him some crackers. Then she would bring a stool over to the refrigerator, climb up to the freezer, and get out two ice cubes. These she would wrap carefully in a washcloth and take to her mother, who would be on the couch, crying. Usually her mother accepted the healing gift in silence, with a half smile and a hug. Then Shelly would go back to the kitchen to make dinner—macaroni and cheese or peanut butter sandwiches. That was all she knew how to make, but Bobby liked both and cleaned his plate every time.

Now Shelly could see their old house. Her glance went quickly to the driveway. She was relieved not to see her father's car, but she still wished she didn't have to come back. She was furious at the reason they were there. As a Brownie Scout, Shelly had taken orders for Girl Scout cookies. But her scout leader had refused to send the cookies to the apartment where Shelly and her mother and brother were staying with a friend. The scout leader said she didn't approve of divorce—she personally believed a family should stay together at home. So that's where she had sent the cookies —to Shelly's old house!

Shelly couldn't believe how stupid and mean that was. She was glad her mom had had enough courage to get help from a lawyer and start divorce proceedings. On the way over, her mother had said that her father would probably have received the notice about the divorce yesterday. That Brownie leader was an idiot! Shelly shook her head. She didn't want to be here, but she had written down the orders of all those teachers at school. The teachers had already paid her. She had to deliver their cookies.

Slowly they all got out of the car, and Shelly helped Bobby up the front steps. As their mother fumbled for her keys, the front door swung open, and there stood Shelly's father, smiling. "Have you come home to stay?" he asked. Shelly stammered something about her Girl Scout cookies, and made a beeline for the pile of boxes she could see in the corner of the living room. Her mother and brother followed her in, and her father closed the door, still smiling. As he picked up an important-looking paper from the coffee table, he asked her mother how long she was going to stay at her friend's apartment. Shelly's mother said it depended on when she could get a job. She pointed to the paper and said it was true she wanted a divorce. They couldn't live the way they had been—fighting whenever they were together. No. They were not home to stay—*never* again. As her mother and father started to argue and their voices rose, Shelly felt the familiar fear return. Automatically she dragged Bobby up the stairs to their old room.

The bedroom was a mess, with lumber and tools scattered all about. Shelly stumbled over the piles of wood, carrying Bobby as best as she could. She sat him down in a dark corner behind some lumber and was just crouching beside him when they heard an explosion downstairs. A gun—Shelly knew it was a gun. Her father had once told her that he had a gun locked away. Fear stabbed her stomach. The next sound they heard was footsteps coming up the stairs. Shelly clamped her hand over Bobby's mouth and held him to her. The footsteps came closer.

"Bobby . . . Shelly . . . where are you?" their father called. Shelly's hand tightened over Bobby's mouth. She hugged him for dear life. Don't move, just don't move—she sent the silent plea to him with her body.

"Shelly . . . Bobby . . . where'd you go? Come on out!" More footsteps, closer still. Then, *crash*! Pieces of wood fell to the floor as their father stumbled into the bedroom. "Damn kids!" he yelled.

He stood for a moment, then turned around and went down the stairs.

Shelly and Bobby didn't move. Shelly listened carefully, but she couldn't hear any noise from below. Just as she began to wonder what they should do next, another shot exploded the silence. Then there was nothing. Shelly and Bobby sat frozen together, waiting for the next sound. It seemed like hours to Shelly, but nothing more happened.

Slowly she took her hand away from Bobby's mouth and whispered, "We got to go now." Bobby nodded, his eyes enormous, his body trembling.

Cautiously they made their way out of the bedroom and started down the stairs. They could see their father's legs sprawled at the bottom of the steps. The legs didn't move. Shelly continued on down and carefully stepped over them. Then she lifted Bobby over. She tried to look only at the front door, but she saw white stuff coming out the side of her father's head. She pulled Bobby along faster. As she turned to open the door for her brother, Shelly caught a glimpse of her mother's outstretched arm on the floor, reaching toward the pile of Girl Scout cookies. The boxes were splattered with blood.

Shelly pushed Bobby through the front door and then yanked it shut behind them. "We got to go the Browns' now, Bobby," she told him. He nodded, and Shelly headed toward the neighbors' house, which they could see through the woods. She had walked the path to the Browns' many times before, when her mother had needed to borrow something or when Shelly had just wanted to enjoy the peacefulness of Mrs. Brown's warm, quiet kitchen. It was almost dark now as they trudged through the melting snow in their coats and boots; they hadn't even had a chance to take them off. Shelly took big gulps of the chilly spring air, too shocked to think.

When they reached the Browns', Shelly knocked on the kitchen door. Wiping her hands on her apron, Mrs. Brown opened the door and smiled at the children.

"We got to call 911," Shelly said. "My father shot my mother. He's dead, too." Mrs. Brown's smile vanished. Quickly she pulled the children inside, sat them down at the table, and automatically gave each a gingersnap. After that, she went to the phone. Mr. Brown arrived home from work just in time to hear his wife telling the police something about a shooting. He looked hard at Shelly, then smiled sadly. He ruffled Bobby's hair and went to the sink to wash up.

When Mrs. Brown got off the phone, she met her husband's eyes. "The police will be here soon. We might as well eat."

Shelly was relieved not to have to talk just yet. She looked at the uneaten gingersnap in her hand and put it down. The milk Mrs. Brown handed her with a reassuring smile felt cool and comforting in her dry throat. Shelly sighed deeply and looked at Bobby, who was watching her. She nodded and pointed to the mashed potatoes, and he began to spoon them carefully into his mouth. So did Shelly. At least eating was something familiar and safe.

Fifteen minutes later, blue strobe lights flickered through the woods into the kitchen. There were so many, the snow seemed to turn blue. The on-off/on-off rhythm made Shelly blink. She felt the fear come into her stomach again. When a state trooper and a young woman knocked on the door, Mrs. Brown showed them to the living room. "You wait here while we finish eating," she said firmly. The officials looked surprised, but Mrs. Brown silenced any objections with a quick comment. "Shock needs food. There's plenty of time for talk."

Shelly relaxed a little, smiled her thanks to Mrs. Brown, and took a swallow of her milk. Bobby's face was covered with his dinner, as usual. He looked sleepy. When Shelly had finished, she took a deep breath and whispered to Mrs. Brown, "I'm ready now."

Mrs. Brown picked up Bobby, who rested his head on her shoulder, and together they went into the living room, where the policeman and the young woman were waiting. The blue lights still flashed through the windows as they introduced themselves. "I'm the advocate for families where there has been a shooting," the young woman said. "I will be coming to see you a lot to help you through the changes you'll face. I brought you this." The advocate handed Shelly her old teddy bear from her bedroom. Shelly hugged it tightly and sat down on the couch. Mrs. Brown smiled at her encouragingly and carried Bobby off to put him to sleep in the den.

The advocate sat down next to Shelly. "I'm sorry to have to tell you this, but your mother is dead." Shelly nodded. "And your father is dead, too." Again Shelly nodded. Then she whispered, "I know. They didn't move."

"Can you tell me what happened?" the advocate asked.

"Can you make those blue lights stop?" Shelly said.

"Sure." While the trooper went into the kitchen to make a call on his walkie-talkie, Shelly and the advocate sat together in silence until the blue flashes disappeared. The snow through the window was white again, and the woods were quiet in the moonlight. Shelly took a deep breath, hugged her bear, and started to talk about the last few hours.

"We had to come back to the house to get my Girl Scout cookies," she began. "We thought he wouldn't be there. His car was gone, but he opened the door. He was nice and talking to Mommy about this paper in his hand. Then they started arguing, and Bobby and me went upstairs to our bedroom to hide. That's where we always go."

Shelly looked at the advocate and the trooper and licked her lips. Her throat felt dry again, so she asked for a glass of water. The trooper brought it to her. They waited until she had drunk the water and was ready to go on. "We hid behind the piles of wood for fixing the room. Then something exploded! It was real quiet and we didn't move. Then I heard him coming up the stairs, and I covered Bobby's mouth like this." She put her hand over the teddy bear's mouth and looked him in the eyes with a fearful, silent warning.

"He called us and looked for us. But it was getting dark. He walked into the pile and got hurt and cussed at us. Then he went downstairs. We just kept hiding. Then there was another shot!" Shelly wrapped her arms back around the bear and huddled over the stuffed animal. "It was real quiet for a long time. So I told Bobby, 'We got to go now.' He was real good. He never said a word the whole time. When we got downstairs, I saw my dad's head. There was white stuff coming out of it. We went to the door, and then I saw my mommy lying next to my Girl Scout cookies."

Tears ran down Shelly's cheeks and onto her teddy bear. The advocate hugged Shelly and told her she was doing really well. She asked if Shelly wanted to take a break. Shelly nodded and led the way to the room where Mrs. Brown's grandchildren stayed when they visited. There were some puzzles on a shelf. Shelly took down one with a picture of Noah's ark on the box and dumped the pieces out onto the bed. The advocate helped her find the corners and the straight edges so they could fit the rest of the puzzle together. It was a lot like trying to figure out the puzzle of Shelly's family and what had happened to them. How could there be a family of four people—and then suddenly only two of them were alive? The other half, her parents, were dead. It was too hard to think about. The puzzle was easier.

When they had completed the Noah's ark puzzle, the advocate asked Shelly where their clothes and toys were and where she wanted to stay that night. Shelly looked around the pink room and stroked the lace of the bedspread. She felt safe at the Browns' house, and Bobby was already asleep in the den. So she asked if the state trooper, who was waiting in the living room, could bring their things from the crowded apartment where they had been staying. The advocate smiled. "Oh, yes. The Browns have already offered this room for you and Bobby until we can contact your relatives. Is there anything else I can do for you?"

Shelly looked at the advocate, and her eyes grew large with remembered fear. "My Girl Scout cookies," she whispered. "I've got to deliver my Girl Scout cookies. They paid for them. The teachers at school all bought them from me. They're in the house, next to my mother." The last few words were barely audible.

The advocate nodded and hugged Shelly. "Don't worry about the cookies. Is the list in the bag?" Shelly nodded. "I'll get them from the house. Do you want to deliver them or shall I do it?" Again Shelly nodded and pointed to the advocate.

"I'll make sure they get to the right people," said the advocate. "I know it's important to you. I'll take care of it while you get some rest here. Tomorrow I'll come back and see you."

Shelly relaxed in the advocate's arms and closed her eyes. They sat together for a while. Then the advocate got up and gently laid Shelly down on the bed. Mrs. Brown came in and covered her with the blankets. As they watched the exhausted girl quietly breathing, they wished that somehow this eight-year-old would have a dreamless sleep.

When the advocate went back across the woods to Shelly's house, she found the yard roped off with yellow plastic tape announcing POLICE LINE—DO NOT CROSS. She stepped over the tape and explained who she was to the trooper guarding the door. Inside there were many people busy taking photographs, measuring distances across the floor, stepping carefully around the two bodies. A doctor, who was the police medical examiner, was leaning over Shelly's mother, looking at the bruises on her face.

"I need that pile of Girl Scout cookies. I have to deliver them for the little girl who lived here," the advocate said to the doctor.

The room was suddenly quiet. Everyone turned to look at the advocate, who repeated her request. The police captain in charge, standing behind the doctor, cleared his throat. "Now look here! You can't come barging into the scene of a crime and take away evidence!"

Suddenly all the fear and anger the advocate had tried not to feel while she was with Shelly flooded through her. The power of her emotions made her face hot, but they also gave her the courage to challenge authority.

"Now *you* look here. A little girl's mother and father are lying at your feet! All that little girl can think about is the reason they came back to this house. And that was for those damn cookies! Now everyone's dead and the cookies are still here. She's got to get them to the people who bought them. It's the only thing we can do to reassure this child that there is a little order left in her life!"

No one said a word. The advocate calmly walked over and picked up the pile of boxes. She tried not to look at the white, lifeless hand lying next to them. With her own hands shaking, she carried the boxes into the kitchen and began sponging splattered blood off the cellophane.

"I've got the cookies, Shelly," she whispered to herself. "I've got the cookies."

The next day, the advocate and Shelly sat on the bed, unpacking a large box the state trooper had brought over from the apartment. As they worked, they went over the story of the previous evening again, this time with the advocate telling it and Shelly correcting her and commenting. When they came to the part where her parents started to argue and she and Bobby fled upstairs, Shelly looked worried.

"They always argued about money. If only I had helped Mommy get a job . . . maybe then Daddy wouldn't have been so mad," she said, fear and doubt in her eyes.

The advocate hugged her. "Shelly, this was not your fault. You did a really good job helping your mother when she was hurt from the other fights. And you took such good care of Bobby and yourself by hiding that no one else got hurt. But kids are only supposed to take care of little problems. Big problems like finding jobs and safe homes are for adults to take care of. This terrible thing was not your fault." The advocate knew Shelly would need to hear this many times over in the coming weeks and even years. It would take a long time before she could really believe she was not at fault in the tragedy.

Shelly seemed a little relieved. She began to show the advocate all the presents she had made for her mother. Each construction-paper heart or clay animal she removed from the box was cradled with love and tenderness. Shelly never mentioned her father again to the advocate. The enormity of what he had done and the rage Shelly would eventually experience toward him would come later, after the shock of the first days and weeks was over.

Bobby had not been a talkative two-year-old before the shooting. Since that night, he had been silent. When Shelly and the advocate told him that both his mommy and daddy were dead, he nodded. He wanted to be in Mrs. Brown's lap most of the time, and he went back to sucking his thumb and needing diapers. It probably seemed safer to be a baby again and to be taken care of. The extra care made him feel mothered and reassured, and Bobby needed and deserved that. But at night he was restless and often had bad dreams. So he and Shelly shared a bed, and that seemed to comfort him.

After a week at the Browns' house, Shelly and Bobby moved to their grandparents' home out of state. In shock over the murder of their daughter, they were glad to be able to offer her children—their grandchildren—love and a safe retreat. When Shelly and the advocate said good-bye, the advocate told Shelly, "Your job now is to be a *kid*. You deserve to grow up safe, and to be loved. Remember your mother and all her love for you."

Because Shelly's father had killed himself after he killed her mother, there would be no murder trial. The murderer was dead.

If he had survived, Shelly, as the main witness to the crime, would have had to endure a one- to two-year-long legal process. Some children do have to testify against their parents, and this can be a frightening, overwhelming experience.

If that had happened to Shelly, the advocate she met the night of the murder would have been with her to help her throughout the process. First, the advocate would have explained that she had to see her father again, in court. "How does that feel to you? You don't have to be afraid of him, because he's afraid of you—of your telling the truth. The truth will make you feel strong."

The advocate might have asked, "Are you afraid you will get him in trouble? He is in trouble now. The truth will help the judge decide what punishment and what help he needs in his life." Together they would have explored what else might scare Shelly about seeing her father, about being part of a trial, and they would figure out how to help her cope with it.

Luckily Shelly didn't have to go through a trial, but the children who do are usually assigned an advocate who prepares them for the process. Before the trial, the advocate takes the child or adolescent to the empty courtroom, where he or she can sit in the judge's chair, the jury box, the prosecutor's seat, and the defendant's seat. The advocate explains what each person does at the trial. Then the youth takes the witness stand, and they rehearse the oath. Every witness must swear on a Bible that what he or she says is the whole truth and nothing but the truth, "so help me God."

The advocate makes sure there is a kid's chair on the stand so that the young witness can easily reach the microphone. Together they might test the microphone, playing with the sound a little. Then they would go over the young witness's testimony—how she or he will tell what happened. The advocate asks the kinds of questions the judge and the attorneys might ask, such as "Did your mother have a gun?" "Did she ever hit your father?" In that way, the child won't be surprised or confused by the questions at the trial. Such a visit helps make the courtroom a more familiar place so that on the difficult day of the trial, the child or adolescent can feel a little more comfortable and confident.

On the trial day, the advocate waits outside the courtroom with the young witness. This wait can take hours, depending on how long the other witnesses are examined. Together they might play quiet games or draw pictures or read. Sometimes reporters gather at a trial, to ask witnesses a lot of hard questions. In that case the advocate might find a safe and private place, away from the hubbub.

The advocate who helped Shelly the night of the murder and in the days afterward works with other young witnesses as well. She always asks them if they have a favorite small stuffed animal or other toy that they want to bring with them into the courtroom. She also has a lucky charm that she uses during a trial. Just before the youth takes the stand, she hands over the lucky charm. "I give this to all the young people I work with who have to testify," she says. "Hang onto it tightly when you are on the witness stand. It will give you the strength to tell the truth. *It has never failed yet!*" This reassures a young person that he or she is not alone, that other kids have also endured a trial and given testimony, and have succeeded. It helps young witnesses call on the power and ability within themselves to tell the truth as best they can.

Even when kids feel they have done their best, they can still be angry or upset by some of the questions asked during their testimony. No child likes to describe one parent hurting another. Reliving that can be frightening—and doing so in public is all the more scary and humiliating. Talking about a parent's violent behavior is particularly difficult with the parent watching.

Afterward, the child or adolescent may feel overwhelmed by anger and frustration. If so, the advocate will encourage the witness to go for a walk or throw a hard ball against a wall to release those residual feelings.

Sometimes the verdict, or outcome of a trial, is not what the surviving family wants. They feel the murderer did not get the punishment he deserved. Or they expect to feel better after the verdict, but they don't. The trial, after all, doesn't bring back the person who has been killed. A family is left with the pain of missing the dead person, grief that might have been delayed by the business of the trial. In this case, the advocate might suggest support groups or counselors who are trained to deal with a family's desire for vengeance and to help a family heal from a violent loss.

Although Shelly did not have to go through the additional difficulty of a trial, she did have to learn to live with the pain of her father killing her mother and then killing himself. Once she and Bobby were established in the safety of their grandparents' home, Shelly began to explore this deep misfortune with a trained therapist and counselor. The counselor also worked with her grandparents to help them establish comforting routines for Bobby and Shelly, cope with nightmares, and respond to difficult questions.

Shelly's counselor, like others working with traumatized children, may have used puppets, drawings, games, or stories to explore her feelings. They would begin this exploration with the counselor asking Shelly, "What do you think happened that day?" As Shelly told the story from her viewpoint, the counselor would listen carefully, trying to understand how the confusing world of adult emotions and actions appeared to this intelligent youngster.

"Why do you think it happened?" might be the counselor's next question. This would help both Shelly and the counselor discover any responsibility Shelly might feel for the tragedy and the events leading up to it. The counselor would help Shelly sort out her feelings and perceptions into a realistic understanding of what happened to her family.

As Shelly grew to trust her counselor and as enough time passed for the shock of the violence to wear off, Shelly might begin to ask her own questions. "Why did my father do it?" "What did *I* do to make him do it?" People who survive violent situations sometimes feel "survivor's guilt." They wonder why they are still alive when people they love have died. Shelly's feelings of guilt for surviving the tragedy might mingle with her deep wish that her parents could have stopped fighting, that her family could have been a happy one, that—if only things had been different—the outcome could have been avoided. Just as Shelly wondered right after the murder, "If only I had helped Mommy get a job . . ."

The counselor would help Shelly see how truly heroic she was to save herself and Bobby. "Would he have killed me and Bobby, too?" is a question that Shelly will always wonder about. It's okay not to have all the answers, it's the process of asking the questions that is important. One answer is that her father *didn't* kill them. It wasn't Shelly's responsibility to protect others from her father's violence. But Shelly acted with intelligence and courage, hiding her brother and herself. She did a tremendous job of surviving disaster, and her counselor would gently but firmly remind her of this often.

The rage that Shelly might feel months or even years afterward would be part of her healing process. But she might need help identifying what she feels as rage. Overwhelming anger is hard to live with. Often we feel guilty for having it, and so we hide it, even from ourselves. Such anger is often masked by depression, shame, or sadness. With a counselor, Shelly could seek safe ways to express her rage, such as talking about it, participating in sports, pounding clay, throwing pillows, or even tearing up phone books. She might try to give the tragedy more clarity and meaning by writing and illustrating her own life story. She could create a scrapbook of memories and feelings that would give her permission to love the good side of her father, as well as to be angry with him.

Shelly could also focus on the future. She could join a campaign to make handguns illegal. Or she could participate in any other activity that would help turn her loss into something positive for herself and for others. Activities that bring people together out of hardship create feelings of strength and love in us. Through them we make choices about the future, and in that there is growth and hope. Such activities would help Shelly feel truly free to live her life, not just survive in a state of suppressed rage and fear.

After a year or so, the counselor might help Shelly recognize her own healing process by creating a "bravery celebration." This would be a party to which Shelly could invite favorite people from every area of her life. There would be her favorite foods, decorations, entertainment. The counselor would give a speech about Shelly's heroism in saving her brother and herself from disaster, and her bravery in finding a healing, non-self-destructive way to live with the loss of her mother and father. The counselor would give Shelly an official certificate recognizing her courage in handling the most severe of life's crises. The applause and love that would surround Shelly would help her to congratulate herself on her journey toward a whole future.

Although Bobby was just two years old when his parents died, he was affected by the murder in many ways: by his father's angry voice on that day; by Shelly's panic as she clamped her hand over his mouth and held him close; by the explosions downstairs; and of course by the sight of his dead parents. The strong feelings of others around him, the sudden changes in his routines, and the continued absence of his parents told him that something was unmistakably wrong. Because he was immediately taken care of by loving people, Bobby was able to adjust to a new life fairly smoothly. But he was likely to have tantrums over the smallest loss or whenever anything had to be taken away from him.

As he grows up, Bobby will need to be told the story of what happened to his family many times. It's a hard story to hear, and he'll need to explore its meaning in his own way. He will look at family photographs and notice that it is easier for everyone to talk about his mother than his father. Yet his father will be an important figure in Bobby's imagination. He may wonder what his father was really like, whether he resembles him, and if he has a violent temper like his father. Bobby may be a father himself one day, and feel renewed anger that his own father could abandon a two-year-old son. He may have a few vivid memories of that day or he may have none. But the events that took place that cold spring afternoon are forever part of Bobby's history. Like Shelly, he will need help with his own healing process.

Many children who have been exposed to violent death have trouble feeling safe in their homes, especially at night. It is important for a child to develop his own safety ritual and follow it every night to gain a sense of control and security. This ritual might include using a special flashlight or even wearing a hard hat with a lamp on it, such as miners use, to check the locks on doors and windows and to explore areas that might be especially frightening to the child, like the attic or basement. This physical process will be more reassuring than the best-intentioned words.

With their grandparents and supporters, Bobby and Shelly might create a ritual that would help them say good-by to their parents. They could light special candles every Christmas, on their parents' birthdays, and on the anniversary of their deaths. This could be a way to remember the spirit of love their parents, however imperfectly, tried to give their children. Separately and together, Bobby and Shelly will learn that to reach out for help and express their emotions creatively will enable them to find understanding, acceptance, and the love of others and themselves. This is the love that will heal them.

■ CREATIVE SURVIVAL STRATEGIES

Do you ever feel intimidated by authority? Have you been afraid to go into the principal's office to face a difficult situation? Or into a theater to audition for a play? Or into a classroom to take a test? Or to approach a policeman to get or give information? Or into a courtroom where your parents are being divorced? These moments can be paralyzing. Make yourself a special lucky charm that you can carry with you. Squeeze it when you are nervous. It will help you focus your energy.

People in many countries around the world use worry beads made of seeds or clay or glass that can be fingered when they are nervous. You can make your own. At art supply stores you can buy special clay that bakes at a low temperature in your own oven. It comes in small packages of many colors and can easily be rolled into bead shapes, pierced with a paper clip, and baked on a pie plate for fifteen minutes. When the beads are cool, thread them together with dental floss that is strong and waxed.

You can also try meditative breathing and visualization to help you through hard situations. Take a deep breath, blow it out through your mouth quietly and gently. . . . Then take another and blow. . . . As you keep breathing deeply, allow a picture to form in your mind of a place you find beautiful and peaceful. Then remember what you want to achieve and repeat it to yourself. "I can do this. . . . I can do this. . . ." Oxygen helps dissolve worry, so the more slowly and deeply you breathe, the more calm and less overwhelmed you will feel. Your lucky charm or worry beads in your hand can remind you to breathe, to focus your energy in order to achieve your purpose.

■ FURTHER EXPLORATIONS

A young boy's concern for the safety of his former baby-sitter exposes him to the violence of physical abuse in Betsy Byars's *Cracker Jackson*. Cracker and his friend try to help her to escape, but they fail. Eventually they are aided by Cracker's mother in this compassionate and often humorous story of complex issues.

One of the rewards of writing this book has been the opportunity to be back in touch with the children and teenagers whose stories I've told here. They are older now—some are even working and living on their own. Although it is not customary for counselors to stay in contact with their clients once counseling has been brought to a close, with hospice families ties tend to continue because of the personal histories and intimate moments that are shared in a home setting. Some families I easily rediscovered. Others took months of searching. And a few could not be found at all. What follows is a glimpse of how life has progressed for them since our encounters with death and survival.   .

■ CHAPTER ONE

Liam is now seven years old and has a five-year-old brother, Dylan, and a three-year-old sister, Emma. Although Mac died long before they were born, Dylan and Emma often look at photographs of "their" dog and talk about missing him. One day, when Emma was two, she became very angry with Liam and hit him. "I'm mad at you, Liam! You didn't share Mac!" she shouted. It is possible to grieve over something you never had, and that was part of Emma's anger. The other part, of course, was Emma's normal sibling rivalry.

Liam's family still has not gotten a new dog. Replacing a pet is something that must feel right to a family, whether it takes three months or three years. Every time this family thought about getting another dog, a new baby came along, so instead they got fish as pets (which were less work). Soon all three children will be old enough to care for a dog themselves. They are looking forward to having one to love and plan to name it "Max."

■ CHAPTER TWO

Erik is now eleven years old and an enthusiastic athlete, involved in basketball, football, baseball, and soccer. His sister Kelly is in college, studying to become a police officer. When Erik read his chapter, it brought back many memories of his grandmother and her death. He says he is not troubled by nightmares, although he still doesn't like to sleep in his room. He prefers to sleep in the den, the living room, his parents' room, his sister's room, almost anywhere but his own, except when a friend spends the night. Many children sleep with their parents after a death in the family. It helps them feel safe, and it is an attempt to make sure that other family members don't disappear, too. Sometimes a young person returns to sleeping in his or her own bed by first sleeping in a sleeping bag at the foot of the parents' bed, then sleeping in the bag outside in the hall, and then eventually going back to the room. This worked only partially for Erik. Wherever he chooses to sleep, his family tries to accommodate his wishes.

■ CHAPTER THREE

Lori is twenty-two, finishing college and planning to go on to law school to specialize in criminal law, an interest her father had but was never able to pursue. She said her chapter brought up strong feelings. She still experiences anger over losing her dad at such a young age and being left with so few memories of him. Drawing to express her feelings about him and his illness did not give her any easy solutions to her grief, which was accentuated because she was the youngest and the only girl in her family.

Barry, four years older than Lori, was able to remember almost everything the chapter raised. He is a graduate student now, hoping to become a social worker and help children who lose a parent, as he did. This is the message he wanted to pass on to other kids going through a similar loss.

> *My dad died when I was twelve years old. I am twenty-five now. Not a day goes by I don't think of him. I still feel frustrated that he is not here to share in my experiences, triumphs, and concerns.*
>
> *If you have had this loss, the pain you feel will bring you closer to your heart: the one place where he lives now. It is*

the place where your closest relationship with him exists. Your life is going to bring you pain and confusion for a long time. Focus on the wonderful memories of your dad and the feelings of anger that you may have toward him.

The greatest gift you can give your dad and yourself is to stay in touch with your heart. That is where your dad lives now. It is the only place he will live forever.

If you look away from your heart then you leave him alone, you leave the most essential part of you all alone. Open your heart up to how you feel and express your feelings in any way which you feel comfortable; through song, through art, through sports, or through poetry; anything. In this, your dad will live forever.

■ CHAPTER FOUR

David is finishing his bachelor's degree after some delay, and soon will begin teaching elementary school children. He writes, "I haven't felt much deep pain about my mother in a long time. I feel the experience has helped me to adjust to the idea of people passing over. Her parents [David's grandparents] have passed in the last few years, and my friend is dealing with AIDS and issues of dying now."

■ CHAPTER FIVE

Three years ago, Amy and Betsy watched their brother Billy die in a hospice. His symptoms were nearly the same as Frankie's, and as a result of the unusual coincidence, a surprising and sad discovery was made. The members of the family were victims of a rare genetic disease. What had shown up as a brain tumor in Frankie's tests was now understood to be the manifestation of this genetic disorder. Amy and Betsy's mother, who had appeared to suffer from the symptoms of multiple sclerosis for nine years, was diagnosed with the same disease through sophisticated genetic testing. Both Amy and Betsy have also been tested and have been told they are carriers of a recessive gene that causes parts of the brain to deteriorate.

Betsy has moved out of state and broken communications with her family, so I could not reach her to give her this chapter. She has apparently married and had a baby, whose health is unknown to her sister, Amy. Perhaps she is seeking to put so much pain behind her and start her life over again.

Amy and her mother read this chapter together at a New Year's Eve ceremony and found that it brought back many details of Frankie's last days. Amy is twenty-two now and working three jobs to make ends meet for herself and her mother. She has struggled hard to complete her high school equivalency program and hopes to go to college someday and become a physical therapist. Amy is glad that Billy got to know her as an adult before he died, since Frankie did not. That gives her some peace and resolution in the face of her family's many separations. She says that when she doodles at work, she still draws the same little girl—with no arms, no hands, and no face. Amy feels that if she could graduate from college and break with a past that was out of control, that little lost girl might finally look up and have a face to show the world.

■ CHAPTER SIX

Rose has been working at a small printing company for the four years since she graduated from high school. She provides for her mother and enjoys the freedom that learning to drive and having her own car have given her. She expresses her creativity in ceramics classes and works in other craft media whenever she gets the opportunity. Remembering her father, she wonders why he waited until he was sick to be kind to the family and to act like a real father to her. Rose believes his abuse, and his cancer, were a waste of his life. She misses him, but she admits she feels safer now that he is gone. After two difficult relationships with young men her age, she now prefers the companionship of an older man who is responsible and treats her with respect, kindness, and maturity.

■ CHAPTER SEVEN

Jesse survived many foster homes and reached the age of twenty-one, only to have her life threatened by breast cancer. Following surgery, she underwent chemotherapy; she says she feels better now that her hair is growing back and her strength is returning. She was invited by the Department of Social Services, which had placed her in a succession of foster homes, to talk to foster parents about how to handle adolescents as angry as she was. Jess (as she prefers to be called) has used her anger creatively to help other foster children make a better adjustment than she was able to. She has a loving relationship with her boyfriend, who lives with her and helps care for her during cancer treatments. When she is well enough, Jess finds satisfaction working with the elderly in a nursing home.

But she is still troubled by her past. Jess says that she wishes she could tell her mother how hateful she was, ask her how she dared leave her children and rob them of their childhood. "Even today, I truly do not understand why or what happened that night, or why I am still not able to go through the motions of grieving. . . . The only thing I can say to anyone is never build walls around yourself or you may lose more than a loved one, and that is truly more of a loss and a grief than anything."

Renee is completing high school and happy to be living in the same loving foster home she has been in since four months after her mother died. Gabe shared that foster home with Renee and three years ago finished high school. Then he joined the Merchant Marine and now travels most of the time. He still finds an escape in science fiction.

Jess wrote this poem for the book and dedicated it to her brother, Gabe, and sister, Renee.

> *As I grow older I look back to see*
> *Old priceless pictures of you and me.*

Trinkets and memories of what was
And what can be.

Familiar smiles,
Letters sent from many miles.

As I look back and see
Laughter shared between you and me,
Pain and tears we knew so well,
Anger we shared when we did yell.

But all in all we made it through,
And I know I couldn't have done this
Without you.

As I grow older, wiser
I feel about things as love, hate,
Anger, pain and sorrow.

I'm tired now so maybe
I'll look back some more tomorrow . . .

Even though Jess's good-byes to her mother are still undone, she believes she is ready to move from the anger and blame she has felt for years to acceptance of the way things happen. She wants to try to enjoy the rest of her life.

■ CHAPTER EIGHT

Jessica, Jason, and David read this chapter with their mother. It has been ten years since their dad died. The two families, both suffering losses from cancer, blended well. Jessica is in college now. She has clear memories of her dad's illness and the art sessions at her house. She has been unable to revisit her father's grave, even though she has made the cross-country trip for that purpose three times. Through counseling, she is exploring her feelings and the meaning of her experiences.

Jason's reaction to seeing his drawings again was "WOW! I was angry and violent!" Two years after his father died, Jason and a friend fell down a large drainage pipe and were trapped for hours while classmates and teachers tried to rescue them. Jason spent several days in the hospital, an ordeal that brought back terrible memories for the family, but he recovered fully. He is now a sophomore in college, studying prelaw. He wants to become a lawyer, as his father was.

David was so young when his father died he has just a few foggy memories of him, and he regrets this. But his stepfather filled a void for him. David is a good student, works as a model, and during high school spent a year in France (where, he says, he wanted to stay forever).

All the children, though grown, continue to express their sense of deep loss over their dad, wondering what he would think of their unfolding lives. Jason says he feels that absence more than ever as he becomes a young man in his own right. He wonders how his dad might counsel him, share with him, and grow with him.

■ CHAPTER NINE

Niki is now eight years old. She has been adopted into the family of her mother's brother, his wife, and their two children, who are the same ages as Niki and Angie. Her grandparents and other family members felt it was better for Niki to grow up surrounded by children in a healthy, happy family. All the members of the extended family live within a half hour of one another; Niki continues to feel well connected, cherished, and loved. Two more babies have been born into her adoptive family since Niki arrived, bringing much joy after incredible tragedy.

The family helps her remember the good times, and, as she grows up, understand more about the illnesses of AIDS and alcoholism. Niki has a special chest filled with her mother's favorite dress, photographs, Angie's toys, and tokens of her father, which she opens and explores whenever she wishes.

Despite three heart attacks, Niki's grandmother has dedicated much of her energy to educating people about AIDS and helping to raise funds for research on children with AIDS. Angie's death troubles Ma the most because she feels Angie never got a chance to live, never had a day in her life free from pain. Ma's anger toward Doug, the children's father, used to be voiced as a threat: "When I get to heaven, Doug, you better have your running shoes on, because I'm coming after you!" Now she's grown to have more compassion for him, to see Doug as a victim of AIDS also.

■ CHAPTER TEN

It has been five years since Molly died. Her parents have divorced, and her father has custody of Molly's brother and sister. The family's many problems have been accentuated by grief, and more help and counseling have been offered by the school and other agencies. At Molly's school, there is a bench on the playground with her name on it, with flowers nearby. Over the years, as teachers and students have dealt with the accidental stabbing of a father by his teenage son, as well as other tragedies, they have remembered and used what they learned about loss and grief when Molly died.

Every year, Catherine's school holds grief groups for kids, run by the guidance counselors. These are available to help children deal with the deaths of parents, grandparents, and others whom they love. The staff has also taught several other schools how to handle an expected death, how to anticipate the problems and respond to them before they become crises for the students.

Jackie's friends have grown up and gone to college. They have struggled with their separate griefs, but there have been no more suicides. They are all alive.

■ CHAPTER ELEVEN

Shelly is now eleven, and Bobby is five. They are still living with their grandparents and seem to be thriving in a town where they have many supports. Shelly saw a therapist for a year after the murder, but then asked to stop. She knows help will be available as she grows older, when she may wish to explore those issues again. Christmases are still hard for the family, when the first snow reminds them of the snow on the ground that tragic, early spring day. Shelly dropped out of Girl Scouts, angry with the Brownie leader and saddened by the memory of the cookies. Bobby still reacts strongly anytime something is taken away from him or he loses something. But the many photos on the walls and the happy stories told to the children by their grandparents help Shelly and Bobby absorb their past in a positive way and enjoy their lives in the present.

Virginia Lynn Fry is an artist and counselor who has worked with dying people and their families for over fourteen years, creating many bereavement groups for children and adults. She is the director of the Hospice Council of Vermont and is a bereavement counselor with the hospice in Montpelier, where she lives with her husband and three children. Ms. Fry teaches at the University of Vermont, travels, and lectures extensively about her experiences linking human creativity with life and death crises and developmental changes.